One can eat—or give away—only so many jams or pickles on their own. Marisa has not only given me delicious destinations for my garden creations, but also justification for planting and preserving more!

—MARTHA HOLMBERG,
coauthor of *Six Seasons*

⸻

Instead of letting jams and pickles languish in your fridge (guilty), you could be using them to lacquer chicken wings, swirl into pancakes, and perk up salad dressings. Marisa McClellan gives us the nudge and the tools we need to liven up our cooking, just by remembering the powerhouses we have waiting in the fridge door.

KRISTEN MIGLORE,
author of *Genius Recipes* and *Genius Desserts*

⸻

Marisa has been our expert guide, leading us deep into the canning pantry; now she is putting us and our jam (and pickles! and chutney!) to work in the kitchen. From sweets to meat, booze to biscuits, this is a massive collection of accessible, delicious, and homemade kitchen staples and comfort foods worthy of your homemade preserves. Buy this book for yourself and the canning enthusiasts in your life.

—KAREN SOLOMON,
author of *Asian Pickles* and *Jam It, Pickle It, Cure It*

THE
food *in* jars
KITCHEN

140 WAYS TO COOK, BAKE, PLATE, AND SHARE YOUR HOMEMADE PANTRY

⁓

MARISA McCLELLAN

RUNNING PRESS
PHILADELPHIA

Running Press
Hachette Book Group
1290 Avenue of the Americas, New York, NY 10104
www.runningpress.com
@Running_Press

Printed in China

First Edition: April 2019

Published by Running Press, an imprint of Perseus Books, LLC, a subsidiary
of Hachette Book Group, Inc. The Running Press name and logo is a trademark
of the Hachette Book Group.

The Hachette Speakers Bureau provides a wide range of authors for speaking events.
To find out more, go to www.hachettespeakersbureau.com or call (866) 376-6591.

The publisher is not responsible for websites (or their content) that are not
owned by the publisher.

Print book cover and interior design by Amanda Richmond.
Food and prop styling by Erin McDowell.

Library of Congress Control Number: 2018946737

ISBNs: 978-0-7624-9246-6 (hardcover), 978-0-7624-9245-9 (ebook)

RRD-S

10 9 8 7 6 5 4 3 2 1

This book is dedicated to my sister, Raina,
whose wild creativity and love are
gifts I will never stop appreciating.

CONTENTS

INTRODUCTION

LET ME TELL YOU ABOUT A CONVERSATION I'VE HAD REPEATEDLY over the years with my friends, neighbors, blog readers, canning students, and anyone else who learns what I do for a living. After a moment or two of chatting, they begin to confess that they love canning, but have trouble using up the contents of their homemade pantry. With a resigned shrug, they say, "After all, I can only eat so much toast."

Once I hear that, I leap into the conversation and quickly rattle off half a dozen ways that I use my preserves beyond toast. I tell them how to combine aromatic vegetables, fresh or dried herbs, vinegar, and jam to create a quick sweet-and-sour braising medium for meat and poultry. I describe a savory goat cheese tart featuring tomato or onion jam.

I talk them through various salads and side dishes that incorporate diced pickles and mustard vinaigrettes. We contemplate all the ways one can combine preserves with yogurt to create parfaits, dips, sauces, and spreads. Without fail, they go off brimming with ideas and feeling like their collection of jams and pickles is an asset rather than a millstone.

When I first started writing about canning and preserving and teaching classes on the subject, I thought my mission ended once my readers and students understood the mechanics of the boiling water bath. I believed that once people had a full pantry, they'd be well on their way to a more independent and homemade life.

However, I quickly discovered that I was wrong. I see now that my job is to help people complete the circle. You may have heard of the concept of cradle-to-grave design. I think of this as empty-jar-to-empty-jar education. I want everyone to understand and be able to embrace the full lifecycle of a jar of jam, jelly, chutney, or pickles. I believe that a pantry full of homemade jams, jellies, salsas, and pickles is a boon, a gateway to easy home cooking and tasty baked goods, and a huge help when it comes to entertaining creatively.

The mission of this book is to show you how to take your various preserves well beyond the typical applications, with both flexible formulas and step-by-step blueprints. The recipes included in this volume have been designed so that they don't require specific preserves to work. Instead, they call for things like a cup of unsweetened applesauce, half a cup of runny berry jam, or two tablespoons of chopped pickles. That is by design, to give you optimum flexibility so as to use up the contents of your individual pantry (whether homemade, gifted, or bought at a farmers' market or grocery store).

Because there will always be some variability between the jams that I make and the ones in your pantry, these recipes have been cross-tested by a panel of home cooks and canners with a variety of homemade and store-bought preserves, all with an eye toward pinning down any issues that may arise and making the recipes as foolproof as possible. Some of the recipes include a lot of narrative instruction as a result. Please do read the recipes carefully and thoroughly before diving in, so that your process can be informed by our hard collective work.

Much of the food in this book is the kind that many of us ate as kids. It's home cooked, cozy, and occasionally homely. While there are plenty of things that are worthy of a dinner party, the fact of the matter is that when you're working with various jams, chutneys, and fruit butters, the end result is often a dish of delicious food in varying shades of brown. I embrace this aspect of these dishes because it recalls earlier times, when everything on the table was homemade, homegrown, or local, out of necessity rather than trend. To borrow a phrase from the engineering trade, it's a feature, not a bug.

EQUIPMENT

THE RECIPES IN THIS BOOK ARE, FOR THE MOST PART, BASIC HOME cooking. If you have a kitchen with a fairly conventional set of cookware and tools, you should be ready to put this book through its paces. There are a few things I do want to call out especially, as I use them a lot in these pages and you might not already have them.

Rimmed baking sheets in 18 x 13 inch/46 x 33 cm and 13 x 9 inch/33 x 22 cm, otherwise known as half and quarter sheet pans, respectively. Not a day goes by when I don't reach for one or the other. The quarter sheet pans are what I use to bake the Shortbread Bars (page 139), Linzer Bar Cookies (page 146), and most vitally, the Jam Slab Pie (page 178).

Removable bottom tart pans. These are used in the Pies and Tarts section (page 174) and will make your homemade tarts look beautiful and professional.

Springform pan. Nothing works as well as this pan for the Flourless Chocolate Cake (page 162).

Offset spatula. I like the smaller versions of these handy tools. Best thing around for smoothing cake batter in the pan.

Silicone spatulas. Everyone has a favorite stirring tool and mine are fully encased silicone spatulas that can go in the dishwasher. I have several so that there's always a clean one when I need it.

Measuring cups. A nesting set of graduated measuring cups and a few large-capacity plastic or glass measuring cups will always be useful.

A digital scale. There's no piece of kitchen gear that I reach for more than my OXO 11-pound/5 kg capacity digital scale.

Immersion blender. Purée soups and sauces without having to clean a food processor bowl or blender container!

Cookie scoops. I have them in 1- and 3-tablespoon sizes and could not love them more.

Beyond those things, there are a few tools that are nice to have that I will reference on occasion in these recipes. Included in that list are a few sharp knives of various sizes, a sturdy peeler, a rasp-style zester, and a fine-mesh strainer.

BREAKFAST
AND BRUNCH

Conventionally, morning meals are where jams, jellies, fruit butters, and other sweet spreads do the bulk of their heavy lifting. Truth be told, most of us know how to spread jelly on toast, sweeten plain yogurt with runny jam, or enhance bowls of oatmeal with apple butter, so I'm not going to rehash any of that well-traveled ground.

I could have filled this entire book with things designed for breakfast and brunch, so I spent a lot of time working to make this section a collection of morning all-stars. There were a few things that didn't make the cut, because I felt that they'd be too much of a turnoff (the jelly omelets I loved as a kid spring immediately to mind) or too trendy to be timeless. If I did my job right, you'll find a number of enduring morning dishes in the following pages.

FRUIT BUTTER BAKED OATMEAL

SERVES 6 TO 8

The first time I encountered baked oatmeal was at a bed-and-breakfast in Harrisburg, Pennsylvania. Studded with frozen blueberries, it managed to be simultaneously soggy and unpleasantly dry. However, I was intrigued by the concept of an oatmeal dish that could be made over a weekend and sliced and reheated throughout the work week, so I got to work creating my own. The result is slightly cakey, and with a splash of milk, it microwaves beautifully.

RECOMMENDED PRESERVES: *Any fruit butter will do. I've tried it with apple, plum, and pear and they were all delicious.*

Nonstick spray or unsalted butter for pan

2½ cups/250 g rolled oats, divided

1 cup/120 g chopped pecans, lightly toasted

½ cup/85 g golden raisins

1 teaspoon baking powder

1 teaspoon ground cinnamon

½ teaspoon fine sea salt

1¼ cups/300 ml milk

2 large eggs

1 cup/240 ml fruit butter

1 teaspoon vanilla extract

¼ cup/50 g granulated sugar

1 cup/240 ml water

Preheat the oven to 375°F/190°C. Spray an 8-inch/20 cm square baking dish with nonstick spray.

Place 1 cup/100 g of the oats in a blender and pulse until the oats are broken down into a rough flour.

Combine the oat flour in a large bowl with the remaining 1½ cups/150 g of rolled oats and the pecans, raisins, baking powder, cinnamon, and salt.

Place the milk, eggs, fruit butter, vanilla, sugar, and water in the same blender container (no need to wash). Blend until well combined.

Pour the liquid from the blender into the oat mixture and stir together.

Scrape the batter into the prepared baking dish. Bake until the edges begin to pull away from the pan and the top is golden brown, 40 to 45 minutes.

Serve warm.

OATMEAL APPLESAUCE BARS

MAKES 12 BARS

These bars are morning lifesavers. I suggest that you keep a few in the fridge or freezer for days when you're running late but still want something relatively healthy that can be quickly consumed while you juggle household chaos or your morning commute. Even better is the fact that they are easy to make. All the prep is done in a food processor.

RECOMMENDED PRESERVES:
I like these best with plain applesauce, but they work nicely with peach or pear sauce as well. You could also make them with fruit butter, though in that case, I recommend you reduce the added sugar by 1 to 2 tablespoons.

Nonstick spray

3 cups/300 g rolled oats, divided

1 teaspoon baking soda

½ teaspoon baking powder

1 teaspoon ground cinnamon

½ teaspoon freshly grated nutmeg

½ teaspoon fine sea salt

2 large eggs

1 cup/240 ml applesauce

½ cup/110 g packed brown sugar

4 tablespoons/55 g unsalted butter, melted

1 cup/120 g chopped pecans, walnuts, or almonds, toasted

Preheat the oven to 350°F/177°C. Grease a 13 x 9-inch/33 x 23 cm pan with nonstick spray and line it with parchment paper, leaving the paper ends protruding to overhang on 2 opposite sides.

In the work bowl of a food processor, combine 1½ cups/150 g of the oats and the baking soda, baking powder, cinnamon, nutmeg, and salt. Process until the oats are broken down. Add the eggs, applesauce, brown sugar, and melted butter and process just until the ingredients are well mixed.

Add the remaining 1½ cups/150 g of rolled oats and the toasted nuts, and pulse 5 or 6 times, until the mixture is just combined.

Spread the batter evenly in the prepared pan and bake for 30 to 35 minutes, or until the tops are a golden brown, the corners have begun to pull away from the sides of the pan, and a toothpick inserted in the middle comes out mostly clean.

Remove the oat slab from the oven and let it cool completely before removing from the pan. Once it is cool, use the overhanging parchment paper to lift the slab out of the pan. Slice into 12 equal bars with a serrated knife. Store in an airtight container at room temperature for up to a week. For longer storage, wrap the bars individually, tuck them into a resealable plastic bag, and freeze.

OATMEAL MUFFINS

MAKES 12 MUFFINS

Everyone needs a quick, healthy muffin recipe in their culinary arsenal and this is mine. I like using some fruit butter in place of the more traditional applesauce because it brings added sweetness and tenderness. They're good for easy weekday breakfasts or made in mini-muffin tins for a church coffee hour.

RECOMMENDED PRESERVES:
I've made these with apple, pear, and plum butters. The plum makes them bake up a bit darker than the other two, but all three taste great.

Nonstick spray for muffin pan

1 cup/100 g whole wheat pastry flour

1 cup/100 g rolled oats

2 teaspoons baking powder

2 teaspoons ground cinnamon

½ teaspoon baking soda

½ teaspoon fine sea salt

1 cup/240 ml whole milk

½ cup/100 g firmly packed light brown sugar

1 large egg

¼ cup/60 ml neutral oil

¼ cup/60 ml fruit butter

½ cup/85 g raisins or other dried fruit (optional)

Preheat the oven to 400°F/204°C. Lightly spray a standard 12-cup muffin pan with nonstick spray.

In a medium bowl, stir together the flour, oats, baking powder, cinnamon, baking soda, and salt. In a separate bowl, stir together the milk, brown sugar, egg, oil, and fruit butter.

Stir the wet ingredients into the dry, stirring just until no flour remains visible. If you're adding dried fruit, fold it in now. Let the batter rest for a few minutes, so that the oats can absorb some of the liquid.

Spoon the batter into the prepared muffin pan. Bake for 18 to 20 minutes, or until a toothpick inserted into the center of a muffin comes out clean.

Remove the muffins from the pan and let them cool. Serve warm or at room temperature.

BANANA APPLESAUCE BREAD

MAKES 2 LOAVES

This is the banana bread my mom has been making my whole life. She didn't like the flavor when it was made with all banana, so she lightened it with applesauce. I like to cut inch-wide slices, sandwich sheets of parchment between the slices, and then wrap the whole thing for the freezer. One cycle in the toaster oven and you've got a warm slice of banana applesauce bread that tastes just as if it was freshly baked.

RECOMMENDED PRESERVES:
If you don't have applesauce, try this one with any other unsweetened fruit sauce. Pear is particularly good. If your sauce is sweetened, reduce the sugar in the batter by ¼ cup.

½ cup/110 g neutral oil, plus more for pans

1¾ cups/220 g all-purpose flour

1¾ cups/225 g whole wheat flour

1¼ cups/250 g granulated sugar

1 tablespoon baking powder

1 teaspoon baking soda

1 teaspoon fine sea salt

1 teaspoon ground cinnamon

½ teaspoon ground ginger

½ teaspoon ground allspice

⅛ teaspoon ground cloves

3 large eggs, beaten

1 cup/265 g unsweetened applesauce

1 cup/250 g mashed banana (2 to 3 bananas)

Preheat the oven to 350°F/177°C. Oil two 9 x 5 x 3-inch/23 x 13 x 8 cm loaf pans.

In a large bowl, whisk together the flours, sugar, baking powder, baking soda, salt, cinnamon, ginger, allspice, and cloves.

Add the beaten eggs, applesauce, mashed bananas, and oil and stir until well combined.

Scrape the batter into the prepared loaf pans and bake for 45 to 55 minutes, or until a cake tester inserted into the center of a loaf comes out clean. If the tops start to overbrown before the interiors are set, gently cover with a piece of foil.

Remove the pans from the oven and place them on a wire rack to cool. Once the loaves are nearing room temperature, remove them from their pan and let them finish cooling on the rack.

Tightly wrapped, these loaves will keep on the counter for up to 5 days. For longer storage, refrigerate or freeze.

Note: If you prefer (or if you only have one loaf pan), you can also bake this batter in standard 12-cup greased or lined muffin pans. Muffins will take 20 to 25 minutes to bake.

POPUNDERS

MAKES 12 POPUNDERS

One of the fun things about traditional popovers is that they fill with airy compartments as they bake. But no one needs yet another popover recipe. Instead, I offer my childhood recipe for popunders. These custardy cups don't achieve the same height as their lofty cousins, but in exchange they are the perfect vehicle for preserves both sweet and savory. They also reheat better and can be made in mini-muffin tins and filled. They are especially great as part of an appetizer menu, filled with savory items, such as small spoonfuls of chutney and a few crumbles of cheese.

RECOMMENDED PRESERVES:
Jam or fruit butter. Really anything goes here.

Nonstick spray, for muffin pan
1 cup/240 ml whole milk
2 large eggs
1 cup/120 g all-purpose flour
¾ teaspoon fine sea salt
¼ cup/60 ml jam or chutney

Spray a 12-cup muffin pan thoroughly with nonstick spray.

Combine the milk, eggs, flour, and salt in a blender and purée until smooth, about 30 seconds, scraping the sides down once. Divide the batter evenly in the prepared muffin pan. Each cavity will be about a third of the way full.

Place the muffin pan in a cold oven and set it to 450°F/232°C. Bake until they brown and puff up a bit, 18 to 22 minutes. Try not to open the oven too often to check them, as it slows down the baking time. They should remain concave in the center, but if they do puff all over, know that they will settle back down.

Popunders (and popovers) are best served warm, so plan on serving these as soon as they come out of the oven. If you do have leftovers, they are best reheated in a toaster oven.

If you're serving them all at once, fill each concave center with about 1 teaspoon of jam. If they've puffed more than you'd like, press the centers down with a spoon before filling.

Note: For more traditional popovers with airy lift, preheat the oven prior to baking and divide the batter between just 8 muffin or popover cavities in an oiled, straight-sided muffin pan.

JAM-FILLED BISCUITS

MAKES 8 BISCUITS

These jam-filled biscuits are my version of the ones I used to get at Grand Central Baking in my much younger days. It's an artisanal bakery that started in Seattle and opened its Portland shop during my freshman year of high school. Whenever my friends and I headed for Hawthorne Boulevard to visit Escentials and Buffalo Exchange, we'd end our trip with a treat from Grand Central.

RECOMMENDED PRESERVES: *Strawberry, raspberry, and apricot are my favorites to use here, although any well-set jam can be used.*

3 cups/360 g all-purpose flour, plus more for dusting

1 cup/110 g whole wheat flour

3 tablespoons granulated sugar

2 teaspoons baking powder

1½ teaspoons fine sea salt

1 teaspoon baking soda

8 ounces/225 g cold, unsalted butter, cut into small squares

1¼ cups/300 ml buttermilk, divided

¾ cup/180 ml jam

Preheat the oven to 350°F/177°C. Line a rimmed baking sheet with parchment paper or a silicone baking mat.

Place the flours, sugar, baking powder, salt, and baking soda in the bowl of a stand mixer fitted with a paddle attachment. Stir to combine.

Add the butter to the bowl. Run the mixer on medium speed, just until the butter begins to combine with the flour mixture and the flour mixture starts to look sandy. You want some larger chunks of butter to still remain.

With the mixer off, pour 1 cup/240 ml of buttermilk into the center of the dough mixture. Run the mixer on low speed until the dough begins to come together. Using a silicone spatula, scrape the walls of the bowl and bring the dough together. Add the final ¼ cup/60 ml of buttermilk and run the mixer on low speed again, until the dough incorporates all the liquid. It should be both a little sticky and still have some floury patches. Remember that with all biscuits, the goal is to mix as little as possible to bring the dough together.

Lightly dust your work surface with flour and turn out the dough onto it. Flour your hands and gently work the dough into a large, rough rectangle that's about ½ inch/1.25 cm thick. Using a bench scraper, fold the dough in thirds and pat it into a rectangle that is about 1½ inches/3.8 cm thick and 8 x 5 inches/20 x 13 cm.

Cut the dough into 8 square biscuits, using a very sharp knife. This helps with portioning and keeps you from having to reroll the dough and make it tough.

Carefully make hollows in the biscuits with your thumb and pointer finger, gently pulling the sides up a little to work the jam well into the center of the dough. Do your best not to compress the flaky layers along the sides of the biscuits, because you want them to rise up and help maintain the jam well as the biscuits bake. Spoon a scant tablespoon of jam into each hollow.

Place the pan on the center rack of the oven and bake for 35 to 40 minutes. I like to rotate the pan halfway through baking to ensure that they brown evenly. The jam-filled biscuits are done when they've puffed up a bit, the edges are deeply burnished, and the jam is bubbling but hasn't started to burn.

Remove from the oven and eat as soon as the jam has cooled enough that it won't scorch your fingertips. Store any leftovers in an airtight container on your countertop for up to 3 days. To refresh day-old biscuits, toast for 2 to 3 minutes.

BASIC JAM-STREAKED SCONES

MAKES 8 SCONES

Some say that the scone is the ideal vehicle for jam. And while I agree, I also believe it to be even better when one is able to tuck the jam right into the scone itself. There are two good ways to weave the jam into the dough, though both are a little messy.

In the first method, you divide the dough into two equal portions. You place the first portion on a flour-dusted countertop and roll it out into a circle that is roughly 10 inches/25 cm in diameter. You top that circle with jam and spread out the jam, leaving a narrow perimeter of bare dough around the edges. Then, you roll out the second round to about the same size and plonk it on top. Press the edges together, cut it into wedges, pop them onto a parchment-lined baking sheet, and into the oven they go.

In the second method, roll out the entirety of the dough into a large sheet, spread the jam across the center of the sheet, and then fold the edges into the middle. Flatten gently with a rolling pin, and then the same cutting, transferring, and baking applies.

Note: I typically default to the second technique more than the first because it's generally quicker and I find that with a little practice, it ends up containing the jam a little better. However, the first technique is a bit neater, so if you hate making a mess of your countertops, it might be the approach for you.

RECOMMENDED PRESERVES:
The world is your oyster here. Just about any sweet or savory jam or chutney will work nicely. I like to use something that's on the higher end of the sugar content spectrum, because there's but a scant measure of sugar in the dough.

2 cups/240 g all-purpose flour, plus more for dusting

2 tablespoons granulated sugar

1 tablespoon baking powder

½ teaspoon fine sea salt

Preheat the oven to 375°F/190°C. Line a baking sheet with parchment or a silicone baking mat.

Place the flour, sugar, baking powder, and salt in a medium bowl and whisk to combine.

Cut the butter into small pieces and add it to the bowl. Using your fingers, rub the butter into the flour mixture, until the flour mixture is pebbly with the butter.

Beat the egg in a small bowl and add ½ cup/120 ml of the milk. Gently work the wet ingredients into the dry with a fork or wooden spoon. Add more liquid, a tablespoon at a time, as needed. You want the dough to be dry enough that you can pat it out and move it, but not so dry that it doesn't hold together. Dust your countertop with flour and roll out your dough (see headnote to determine which approach you want

6 tablespoons/85 g cold, unsalted butter

1 large egg

½ to ⅔ cup/120 to 160 ml milk, buttermilk, yogurt, or heavy whipping cream

⅓ to ½ cup/80 to 120 ml jam

to take to fill your scones). Fill with the jam of your choosing. If your jam is quite thick, you will want to use a larger portion than if it is runny. Cut the scones into 8 wedges and transfer them to the lined baking sheet.

Bake for 20 to 22 minutes, or until the tops are nicely browned and the scones have achieved some lift. Serve hot.

GINGER MARMALADE SCONES

MAKES 8 SCONES

Although UK residents wouldn't recognize these as traditional scones, they have a decidedly British feel to my American palate. I like to serve them with a strong pot of black tea and more marmalade for topping.

RECOMMENDED PRESERVES:
Classic, thick-cut orange marmalade is great here, as are more esoteric ones, such as kumquat or blood orange.

2 cups/240 g all-purpose flour, plus more for dusting

2 tablespoons granulated sugar

1 tablespoon baking powder

1 teaspoon ground ginger

½ teaspoon fine sea salt

6 tablespoons/85 g cold, unsalted butter

1 large egg

½ cup/120 ml buttermilk, plus more as needed

⅓ cup/80 ml orange or lemon marmalade

2 tablespoons diced crystallized ginger

Preheat the oven to 375°F/190°C. Line a baking sheet with parchment or a silicone baking mat.

Place the flour, sugar, baking powder, ginger, and salt in a medium bowl and whisk to combine.

Cut the butter into small pieces and add it to the bowl. Using your fingers, rub the butter into the flour mixture, until the flour mixture is pebbly with the butter.

Beat the egg in a small bowl and add the buttermilk. Gently work the wet ingredients into the dry with a fork or wooden spoon. Add more liquid, a tablespoon at a time, as needed. You want the dough to be dry enough that you can pat it out and move it, but not so dry that it doesn't hold together. Roll out and fill the scones using your technique of choice (see headnote, page 16). Evenly distribute the crystalized ginger on top of the jam before closing the scones.

Cut the scones into 8 wedges and transfer them to the lined baking sheet.

Bake for 20 to 22 minutes, or until the tops are nicely browned and the scones have achieved some lift.

PEACH WALNUT CREAM SCONES

MAKES 12 SCONES

I think of these scones as the perfect offering for wedding and baby showers. They go well with coffee and mimosas, making them good for both brunch and later day gatherings. Keeping those more dainty events in mind, I like to cut these scones into 12 portions rather than 8, as it makes for a more delicate presentation.

RECOMMENDED PRESERVES:
These are best with peach jam or slightly chunkier peach preserves, but they also work nicely with jams made from nectarines and cherries.

2 cups/240 g all-purpose flour

¼ cup/30 g finely chopped walnuts, lightly toasted

2 tablespoons granulated sugar

1 tablespoon baking powder

½ teaspoon fine sea salt

6 tablespoons/85 g cold, unsalted butter

1 large egg

⅔ cup/160 ml heavy whipping cream, plus more as needed

Place the flour, walnuts, sugar, baking powder, and salt in a medium bowl and whisk to combine.

Cut the butter into small pieces and add it to the bowl. Using your fingers, rub the butter into the flour mixture, until the flour mixture is pebbly with the butter.

Beat the egg and add the cream. Gently work the wet ingredients into the dry with a fork or wooden spoon. Add more liquid, a tablespoon at a time, as needed. You want the dough to be dry enough that you can pat it out and move it, but not so dry that it doesn't hold together. Roll out and fill the scones using your technique of choice (see headnote, page 16). Cut the scones into 12 wedges and transfer them to the lined baking sheet. Bake for 20 to 22 minutes, or until the tops are nicely browned and the scones have achieved some lift.

TOMATO CHEDDAR SCONES

MAKES 12 SCONES

These savory filled scones are my favorite thing to serve alongside a bowl of hearty soup on chilly nights. They're also a really nice item to make for new parents, who often need a quick, handheld snack that isn't bursting with sugar.

RECOMMENDED PRESERVES:
I love these with Tomato Jam (page 219), but they also work well with apple chutney (see page 221) or onion jam.

2 cups/240 g all-purpose flour

2 tablespoons granulated sugar

1 tablespoon baking powder

½ teaspoon fine sea salt

4 tablespoons/55 g cold, unsalted butter

2 ounces/60 g shredded Cheddar cheese

1 large egg

½ cup/120 ml milk, plus more as needed

½ cup/120 ml Tomato Jam (page 219)

Preheat the oven to 375°F/190°C. Line a baking sheet with parchment or a silicone baking mat.

Place the flour, sugar, baking powder, and salt in a medium bowl and whisk to combine.

Cut the butter into small pieces and add it to the bowl. Using your fingers, rub the butter into the flour mixture, until the flour mixture is pebbly with the butter. Add the shredded cheese and work that in as well.

Beat the egg in a small bowl and add the milk. Gently work the wet ingredients into the dry with a fork or wooden spoon. Add more liquid, a tablespoon at a time, as needed. You want the dough to be dry enough that you can pat it out and move it, but not so dry that it doesn't hold together.

Roll out and fill the scones using your technique of choice (see headnote, page 16). Cut the scones into 8 wedges and transfer them to the lined baking sheet. Bake for 20 to 22 minutes, or until the tops are nicely browned and the scones have achieved some lift.

FILLED CRÊPES

MAKES TWELVE FILLED 8-INCH/20 CM CRÊPES

During my childhood summers, we often spent two to three weeks with my grandparents in Philadelphia. Part of the pleasure of those trips was the food. Tutu and Grandpa Sid said yes to nearly every request we made, and so my sister and I got such treats as sugary cereals, water ice, and Pop-Tarts, all things my mom would never buy. They also always had boxes of fruit-filled blintzes in the freezer that Grandpa Sid would fry in butter and serve with a dollop of sour cream. This recipe produces filled crêpes that are very much like those blintzes, but designed to be easy to prepare ahead of time and serve to a crowd.

RECOMMENDED PRESERVES: *Apple, peach, cherry, or blueberry pie filling are my favorite options, but low-sugar, chunky fruit preserves will also work.*

¾ cup/90 g all-purpose flour

2 tablespoons confectioners' sugar

1 teaspoon baking powder

¼ teaspoon fine sea salt

1 cup/240 ml milk

2 large eggs

½ teaspoon vanilla extract

3 tablespoons unsalted butter, melted

2 cups/480 ml pie filling or chunky fruit preserves

Sour cream or Greek yogurt, for serving

Place the flour, confectioners' sugar, baking powder, and salt in a blender container and pulse to combine. Add the milk, eggs, and vanilla and purée to combine.

Let the batter rest for at least 30 minutes before cooking. You can also make it the night before and stash it in a covered jar in the fridge.

When you're ready to cook, brush the bottom of a 13 x 9-inch/32 x 23 cm baking pan with some of the melted butter.

Heat an 8-inch/20 cm nonstick skillet over medium-high heat. Brush the pan with a little bit of the melted butter and pour in a scant ¼ cup/55 ml of the batter. Tilt and swivel the pan so that the batter spreads evenly over the bottom and lower sides of the pan.

Let the crêpe cook until the batter is set and doesn't look at all drippy and the edges begin to pull away from the sides of the pan. This will take 2 to 3 minutes for the first couple of crêpes, and just 60 to 90 seconds as the pan heats up.

Carefully run a thin spatula around the edges of the crêpe to loosen it from the pan and flip it. Let it cook for 15 to 30 seconds on this side. Lift the crêpe out of the pan and onto a plate. Brush the pan again with butter, add another ¼ cup/55 ml of batter, and cook. Repeat this process until all the batter has been used.

As the crêpes cook, lay a finished crêpe on your work surface and spread about 1½ tablespoons of the filling in a line down the middle of the crêpe. Roll up the crêpe around the filling into a tight cylinder and place, seam-side down, in the buttered dish (the crêpe you're currently cooking should be ready to flip now). It will look as if you're building a pan of pale enchiladas.

Once all the crêpes are cooked, filled, and lined up in the baking dish, pour the remaining melted butter over the rolled crêpes. At this point, you can either cover them and refrigerate them for up to 24 hours before serving or broil them immediately. If you do decide to make them in advance, remove the pan from the fridge about an hour before broiling to ensure that they reheat properly.

Just before serving, place the baking dish under the broiler for 3 to 4 minutes, just until they turn golden brown and the butter sizzles.

Serve immediately, topped with a dollop of sour cream or Greek yogurt.

MO'S FAMOUS PANCAKE MIX

MAKES 8½ CUPS/ABOUT 1 KG DRY MIX

When I was growing up, my mom did the bulk of the cooking. My dad's contributions were limited to holiday foods, things cooked on our ancient charcoal-burning hibachi, and Saturday morning pancakes. He worked at IHOP in the early 1970s and hated their white, doughy stacks that left you hungry an hour after eating. He spent years perfecting his own basic pancake mix so that the resulting cakes would be fluffy and filling in a way that those IHOP pancakes were not. For most of my childhood, he would mix up seven or eight batches of pancake mix in the weeks before Christmas, portion it out into containers, and give it to our friends and neighbors. It became so beloved in our community that we started calling it Mo's Famous.

RECOMMENDED PRESERVES:
Any jam, fruit preserve, or fruit butter makes a nice topper for pancakes. For special occasions, I like to warm the jam with some melted better and a splash of bourbon (recipe follows).

3 cups/360 g all-purpose flour

2 cups/225 g whole wheat flour

1½ cups/170 g toasted wheat germ (I like Kretchmer's honey-toasted)

1 cup/140 g fine cornmeal

¾ cup/150 g granulated sugar

3 tablespoons baking powder

1 tablespoon fine sea salt

FOR 16 TO 18 PANCAKES

2 tablespoons neutral oil, plus more for griddle

3 large eggs

1 cup/240 ml milk, plus more as needed

2 cups/200 g pancake mix

Place all the ingredients in a large bowl and gently whisk to combine. Store the mix in a large, airtight container. To extend the life span of the mix, store it in the fridge or freezer.

To cook: Preheat a lightly oiled griddle over medium heat.

Beat the eggs together in a medium bowl until fully blended, and then whisk in the milk and oil. Fold in the dry mix. If it seems too thick, add a splash more milk.

To tell when the griddle has reached a proper temperature, flick a little water onto the griddle from your fingertips. If the water dances in little balls, the griddle is ready.

Spoon about ¼ cup/60 ml of batter onto the griddle; this will make pancakes that are about 4 inches/10 cm in diameter and they will flip and cook more evenly. Cook until bubbles form around the edges of the pancake, 2 to 3 minutes. Flip the pancakes and cook for another 45 to 90 seconds on the other side, or until golden brown all over. Serve buttered and topped with jam.

Note: I sometimes like to fill these pancakes with jam as they cook. To do that, ladle the batter onto the griddle and immediately spoon a small pool of jam into the middle of each pancake. Cover the jam with a thin layer of batter. Flip as normal and cook for an additional 15 to 30 seconds on the second side to ensure that the extra batter cooks thoroughly.

PANCAKE SAUCE

Combine 1 cup/240 ml) of jam with 2 table-spoons of salted butter in a small saucepan. Warm gently over medium heat until the butter melts and combines with the jam. Once it begins to bubble around the edges, I like to add a tablespoon of bourbon. Stir to combine and cook for another 1 to 2 minutes to cook off the alcohol. If you plan on serving to both kids and adults, it's nice to make one batch with booze and another without.

KIMCHI MATZO BREI

SERVES 1 AND CAN BE EASILY DOUBLED

Matzo brei is a dish made from softened matzo, egg, and butter. It's a staple of Jewish home cooking, particularly during the eight days of Passover. However, it's a tasty dish no matter the time of year or your religious affiliation, and it is an easy thing to stir together when you're running low on groceries. The pieces of matzo get tender and just a little chewy as they cook, the kimchi provides heat and freshness, and the eggs hold it all together.

RECOMMENDED PRESERVES:
As the title of the recipe implies, I typically make this with kimchi, but it's also good with sauerkraut.

1 sheet plain matzo

2 large eggs

½ cup/125 g kimchi, drained and chopped

1 tablespoon salted butter

Place a sieve or colander in the sink and break the sheet of matzo into it. You're going for pieces of about 1 inch/2.5 cm in size. Run water over the matzo pieces for 15 to 30 seconds (the amount of water depends on how brittle the matzo is) so that they soften but aren't totally saturated. Let the matzo drain.

Beat the eggs in a small bowl and add the softened matzo. Add the chopped kimchi and stir to combine.

Place the butter in a small, nonstick skillet over medium-high heat. Once it foams, add the egg mixture and cook, stirring, until the eggs are cooked to your liking. Tip the finished brei onto a plate and serve immediately.

Note: While I prefer my matzo brei savory, a sweetened version topped with jam or maple syrup is also traditional. If this direction sounds good to you, leave out the kimchi and proceed as directed, finishing with a drizzle or dollop of something sweet.

SAUERKRAUT FRITTATA

SERVES 4

Sauerkraut and eggs have long been one of my favorite combinations. I often heap a pile of kraut on a plate, top it with a couple of fried eggs, and call it good. When there are more diners to feed or I simply want to up my game, I call on this frittata. It is endlessly flexible, can be served for any meal, and reheats beautifully. In the summer, I often swap cubed zucchini in for the potato for a lighter and more garden-centric version. I like to serve wedges of this frittata with lashings of tomato jam or hot sauce.

RECOMMENDED PRESERVES:
Any stripe of sauerkraut works well here. I particularly like using one that has a lot of added garlic, for an extra-zippy frittata.

2 tablespoons extra-virgin olive oil

½ yellow onion, finely diced

1 cup/150 g diced white potato (aim for ½-inch/1.25 cm dice)

1 cup/240 ml water, plus more as needed

1 cup/200 g drained Basic Sauerkraut (page 227)

½ teaspoon fine sea salt

¼ teaspoon freshly ground black pepper

6 large eggs, beaten

Preheat the oven to 375°F/190°C.

Heat the olive oil in a 10-inch/25 cm nonstick, oven-safe skillet over medium-high heat until it begins to shimmer. Add the onion and cook, stirring, for 3 to 4 minutes, or until they begin to brown. Add the potato and water. Lower the heat to medium, cover the pan, and let the potato cook for 8 to 10 minutes, checking occasionally, until the potato is tender and the water has evaporated. If there's some residual water, uncover the pan and let it boil off. If the water boils off before the potato is tender, add a splash more.

Once the potato is soft, add the sauerkraut, salt, and pepper and stir to combine. Evenly spread out the ingredients in the pan and add the eggs. Using a silicone spatula, work the beaten eggs into the vegetable mixture and give the pan a gentle wiggle to help it settle.

Transfer the pan to the oven and bake for 8 to 10 minutes, or until the top puffs and turns light brown. Switch your oven to the BROIL setting and broil for 1 to 2 minutes, to brown the top of the frittata.

Remove the pan from the oven and let the frittata cool for a minute or two. Slide a silicone spatula around the edges of the pan to loosen the eggs. Transfer the frittata onto a large cutting board and slice into wedges.

Serve hot or warm.

Note: If you have leftover roasted potatoes in the fridge, feel free to use those here.

Jammy Granola

Of all the ideas I've shared over the years designed to help move jams and fruit butters out of their jars, this one might be my favorite. The concept is that instead of using liquid sweetener and spices to coat your oats and nuts before baking, you toss them with a slurry of sweet preserve and just a touch of oil or melted butter before baking.

BASIC JAMMY GRANOLA

MAKES 4 TO 5 CUPS/400 TO 500 G GRANOLA

If you are looking for ways to use the odds and ends of jam you've got in the fridge, this open-ended recipe will be perfect for you.

RECOMMENDED PRESERVES:
Any slightly runny jam or jelly works here. If the preserve you're using is very chunky, I recommend purée-ing it to help smooth it out.

¾ cup/180 ml jam

¼ cup/60 ml neutral oil or melted butter

2 cups/200 g rolled oats

¾ cup/90 g chopped raw nuts

¾ cup/120 g seeds (such as flax, sesame, hemp, chia, or poppy)

½ teaspoon flaky finishing salt

½ cup/90 g dried fruit or chopped crystallized ginger

Preheat the oven to 325°F/163°C and line a rimmed baking sheet with parchment paper.

Combine the jam and oil in a measuring cup. If the jam is very chunky, give it a quick purée with an immersion blender. If it is very stiff and hard to mix, microwave the mixture in 5-second increments on HIGH until soft enough to stir and spread.

In a large bowl, combine the oats, nuts, and seeds. Pour in the jam mixture. Stir until all the ingredients are well integrated.

Spread the mixture on the prepared baking sheet. Bake, stirring at least twice during baking, for 20 to 25 minutes. The granola is done when it has taken on a deep golden color, smells fragrant, and is no longer visibly moist, though it won't look completely dry until it is fully cool.

Remove the granola from the oven and sprinkle on the salt while the granola is still hot. Stir in the dried fruit and let cool completely on the baking sheet. Once it is entirely cool, funnel it into an airtight jar or food storage container. It will keep in the pantry for up to 2 weeks. For longer-term storage, keep the finished granola in the refrigerator.

PEANUT AND BERRY JAM GRANOLA

This version is one of my favorites to serve to kids (and if I know in advance that they can't have peanuts, I'll make a version with all-sunflower products). The flavors are familiar and go really well with vanilla yogurt or milk.

RECOMMENDED PRESERVES:
Strawberry, raspberry, and blueberry jams are all good here.

¾ cup/180 ml berry jam

¼ cup/60 ml peanut oil

2 cups/200 g rolled oats

¾ cup/90 g chopped raw peanuts

¾ cup/120 g raw sunflower seeds

½ teaspoon flaky finishing salt

½ cup/70 g dried strawberries or blueberries

Preheat the oven to 325°F/163°C and line a rimmed baking sheet with parchment paper.

Combine the jam and oil in a measuring cup. If the jam is very chunky, give it a quick purée with an immersion blender. If it is very stiff and hard to mix, microwave the mixture in 5-second increments on HIGH until soft enough to stir and spread.

In a large bowl, combine the oats, peanuts, and sunflower seeds. Pour in the jam mixture. Stir until all the ingredients are well integrated.

Spread the mixture on the prepared baking sheet. Bake for 20 to 25 minutes, stirring at least twice during baking. The granola is done when it has taken on a deep golden color, smells fragrant, and is no longer visibly moist, though it won't look completely dry until it is fully cool.

Remove the granola from the oven and sprinkle on the salt while the granola is still hot. Stir in the dried berries and let cool completely on the baking sheet. Once it is entirely cool, funnel it into an airtight jar or food storage container. It will keep in the pantry for up to 2 weeks. For longer-term storage, keep the finished granola in the refrigerator.

MARMALADE AND MIXED NUT GRANOLA

MAKES 4 TO 5 CUPS/400 TO 500 G GRANOLA

This is a really good granola for snacking and works beautifully as a topping for big green salads (it's even better if you mirror the flavors by adding segmented oranges or clementines to the salad). It's also a nice one to tuck into holiday gift baskets.

RECOMMENDED PRESERVES:
Orange marmalade is really great here (if you don't have any homemade, Bonne Maman makes a tasty one), but you can also use lemon or lime.

¾ cup/180 ml orange marmalade

¼ cup/60 ml melted unsalted butter

2 cups/200 g rolled oats

¾ cup/90 g chopped mixed raw nuts

¾ cup/120 g pumpkin seeds

½ teaspoon flaky finishing salt

½ cup/90 g chopped candied citrus peel

Preheat the oven to 325°F/163°C and line a rimmed baking sheet with parchment paper.

Combine the marmalade and melted butter in a measuring cup. If the marmalade is very chunky, give it a quick purée with an immersion blender. If it is very stiff and hard to mix, microwave the mixture in 5-second increments on HIGH until soft enough to stir and spread.

In a large bowl, combine the oats, nuts, and seeds. Pour in the marmalade mixture. Stir until all the ingredients are well integrated.

Spread the mixture on the prepared baking sheet. Bake for 20 to 25 minutes, stirring at least twice during baking. The granola is done when it has taken on a deep golden color, smells fragrant, and is no longer visibly moist, though it won't look completely dry until it is fully cool.

Remove the granola from the oven and sprinkle on the salt while the granola is still hot. Stir in the candied peel and let cool completely on the baking sheet. Once it is entirely cool, funnel it into an airtight jar or food storage container. It will keep in the pantry for up to 2 weeks. For longer-term storage, keep the finished granola in the refrigerator.

PEAR, GINGER, AND WALNUT GRANOLA

MAKES 4 TO 5 CUPS/400 TO 500 G GRANOLA

This is the granola I make in the fall when the weather cools and the days shorten. I like to layer it with plain yogurt and slices of fresh pear for a tasty, autumnal parfait.

RECOMMENDED PRESERVES:
Pear jam is my favorite here, but if you don't have that in your pantry, apple or pumpkin butter is a delicious alternative.

¾ cup/180 ml pear jam

¼ cup/60 ml sunflower oil

2 cups/200 g rolled oats

1½ cups/180 g raw chopped walnuts

½ teaspoon flaky finishing salt

½ cup/90 g chopped crystallized ginger

Preheat the oven to 325°F/163°C and line a rimmed baking sheet with parchment paper.

Combine the jam and oil in a measuring cup. If the jam is very chunky, give it a quick purée with an immersion blender. If it is very stiff and hard to mix, microwave the mixture in 5-second increments on high until soft enough to stir and spread.

In a large bowl, combine the oats and nuts. Pour in the jam mixture. Stir until all the ingredients are well integrated.

Spread the mixture on the prepared baking sheet. Bake for 20 to 25 minutes, stirring the granola at least twice during baking. The granola is done when it has taken on a deep golden color, smells fragrant, and is no longer visibly moist, though it won't look completely dry until it is fully cool.

Remove the granola from the oven and sprinkle on the salt while the granola is still hot. Stir in the crystallized ginger and let cool completely on the baking sheet. Once it is entirely cool, funnel it into an airtight jar or food storage container. It will keep in the pantry for up to 2 weeks. For longer-term storage, keep the finished granola in the refrigerator.

TOMATO JAM SMOKED PAPRIKA GRANOLA

MAKES 4 TO 5 CUPS/400 TO 500 G GRANOLA

The first time I tasted savory granola, I nearly lost my mind. Since then, I've made it many times and lean on it heavily whenever I need to add crunch and umami to puréed soups, salads, and roasted vegetables.

RECOMMENDED PRESERVES:
Tomato jam is king here, but any savory jam will work.

¾ cup/180 ml Tomato Jam (page 219)

¼ cup/60 ml extra-virgin olive oil

1 tablespoon smoked paprika

2 cups/200 g rolled oats

1 cup/120 g raw chopped almonds

½ cup/80 g mixed sesame and poppy seeds

1 teaspoon flaky finishing salt

½ cup/90 g dried cherry tomatoes

Preheat the oven to 325°F/163°C and line a rimmed baking sheet with parchment paper.

Combine the jam and oil in a measuring cup. If the jam is very chunky, give it a quick purée with an immersion blender. If it is very stiff and hard to mix, microwave the mixture in 5-second increments on HIGH until soft enough to stir and spread. Stir the smoked paprika into the jam mixture.

In a large bowl, combine the oats, almonds, and seeds. Pour in the jam mixture. Stir until all the ingredients are well integrated.

Spread the mixture on the prepared baking sheet. Bake for 20 to 25 minutes, stirring the granola at least twice during baking. The granola is done when it has taken on a deep golden color, smells fragrant, and is no longer visibly moist, though it won't look completely dry until it is fully cool.

Remove the granola from the oven and sprinkle on the salt while the granola is still hot. Stir in the dried tomatoes and let it cool completely on the baking sheet. Once it is entirely cool, funnel it into an airtight jar or food storage container. It will keep in the pantry for up to 2 weeks. For longer-term storage, keep the finished granola in the refrigerator.

SNACKS AND TOASTS

I will be the first to admit that this chapter is something of an odd-ball. It's the place where I tucked all the lovely, tasty bits that didn't quite fit anywhere else. However, it contains a selection of recipes and ideas that I knew this book needed to have. It's in these pages that you'll find a beer, cheese, and relish sauce designed for pouring over toast. Here also is my recipe for glazed nuts made with jam or marmalade instead of the more traditional sugar or maple syrup. There's also a recipe for crackers that I've been making for years and years, and some ideas for ways to fancy up slices of toast. These are the odds and ends I use to help transform my homemade preserves into more cohesive, thoughtful offerings. The glazed nuts do wonders to help pull together a cheeseboard, and if you serve the toasts on a pretty plate, they suddenly become worthy of company.

JAM-GLAZED NUTS

MAKES ABOUT 4 CUPS/960 ML GLAZED NUTS

Knowing how to transform a pound of raw nuts into a pan of toasty glazed nuts is a hugely valuable kitchen skill. They're a good party snack, they're delicious tossed on a big salad, and nothing makes a better hostess gift. Traditionally, people use maple syrup or honey, but I like to make them with my runnier preserves. The jams and marmalades bring flavor along with their sweetness, which means you don't need additional herbs and spices to make them interesting.

RECOMMENDED PRESERVES: *Choose preserves that you'd like to eat on a peanut or almond butter sandwich. My absolute favorite jam to use is pear vanilla, but grape is also wonderful.*

1 pound/450 g raw almonds, peanuts, cashews, walnuts, or pecans (or a combination thereof)

6 tablespoons/90 ml jam or marmalade

2 tablespoons unsalted butter

1½ teaspoons flaky finishing salt

Preheat the oven to 350°F/177°C. Line a large, rimmed baking sheet with parchment paper or a silicone baking mat.

In a large, dry skillet, toast the nuts over medium heat, stirring frequently so that they don't burn.

In a small saucepan, melt the jam and butter together. When the nuts are looking lightly toasted and are smelling nutty, pour the jam mixture over the nuts and toss to coat.

Spread the coated nuts on the prepared baking sheet. Bake for about 10 to 15 minutes, checking regularly, until the bits of glaze have started to brown.

Remove the nuts from the oven and dust them with salt. Let them cool completely so that the glaze has a chance to harden and adhere. Once cool, break apart any nuts that are stuck together.

Store the finished, cooled nuts in an airtight container for up to 1 month.

RAREBIT WITH RELISH

MAKES 6 TO 8 TOASTS

For most of my life, Welsh rarebit was something I only read about in books. It was the sort of thing that Betsy and Tacy (Maud Hart Lovelace forever!) would stir up in a chafing dish. I was a little deflated when I later learned that it was essentially just cheese sauce on toast. However, having now eaten it many times, it's a concoction I highly recommend. If you're avoiding alcohol or want to feed this to children, feel free to swap in milk for the beer.

RECOMMENDED PRESERVES:
I like to stir in a tablespoon or two of pickle relish or chopped dill pickle just before serving. It's also good with a tangy, spicy chutney. Stay away from anything too sweet, as it won't cut the richness of the cheese quite as well.

1 tablespoon salted butter

1 tablespoon all-purpose flour

½ teaspoon Dijon mustard

¼ teaspoon freshly ground black pepper

½ cup/120 ml beer (avoid anything too hoppy and try a stout or porter)

2 tablespoons whole milk

1 cup/120 g grated Cheddar cheese

2 tablespoons well-drained relish or finely chopped pickle

6 to 8 slices toasted bread

Preheat the broiler. Arrange the toasted bread on a rimmed baking sheet.

Melt the butter in a small saucepan over medium heat. Once it foams, add the flour and whisk to combine into a paste consistency. Let the butter and flour cook together, whisking every 15 seconds or so, until the mixture puffs and starts to turn brown, 1 to 2 minutes. Add the mustard and pepper and stir to combine.

While whisking vigorously, pour in the beer. Once incorporated, add the milk and stir to combine. Let the sauce simmer gently over medium heat, whisking regularly, for 2 to 3 minutes, or until it has thickened and coats the back of a spoon nicely. Once the sauce has thickened and looks quite smooth, remove the pan from the heat and stir in the cheese. Finally, stir in the relish (be sure it's well drained because too much acid can curdle the cheese sauce).

Pour the cheesy sauce over the toasted slices of bread. Broil for 2 to 3 minutes, or until the cheese is nicely browned in spots. Serve immediately. If you're making rarebit for a smaller audience, you can top and broil slices of toast one at a time.

The sauce will keep in a jar or container in the fridge for 3 to 4 days. I often make a batch and eat it for lunch over a slice of toast with a big green salad.

Note: For the smoothest sauce, use cheese grated freshly from the block.

CRACKERS

MAKES 40 TO 50 CRACKERS

I started making these crackers during my grad school years. Cheap and pleasing, they made me feel less like I was a slave to my tight budget and more like I was simply clever and plucky. More than ten years on, I still make them regularly because I like them and it now seems ridiculous to spent eight dollars on a similar bag at my local cheese shop.

RECOMMENDED PRESERVES:
If you have a batch of home-made za'atar or hand-chopped salt, herb, and citrus blend, use that instead of the seed topping. In a pinch, the Everything Bagel Seasoning from Trader Joe's is also a really good topping.

1½ cups/180 g all-purpose flour, plus more for dusting

½ cup/55 g whole wheat flour

1 teaspoon fine sea salt

3 tablespoons extra-virgin olive oil

¾ cup/180 ml water, plus more for sprinkling

2 tablespoons sesame seeds

2 tablespoons poppy seeds

1 tablespoon dried rosemary

1 teaspoon flaky finishing salt

Preheat the oven to 450°F/232°C. Line a pair of rimmed baking sheets with parchment paper (I don't recommend that you use silicone baking mats for this dough, because you want a surface on which you can score the crackers, and that can damage those expensive mats).

In a medium mixing bowl, stir together the flours and fine sea salt. Add the olive oil and water and stir to combine with a silicone spatula. When it gets too stiff for the spatula, switch to using your hands. Work the dough until it comes together into a cohesive ball. Cover the bowl with plastic wrap or a damp kitchen towel for 30 minutes. This lets the gluten that developed in the dough during mixing relax so that you'll be able to roll out the crackers more easily.

In a small bowl, stir together the sesame seeds, poppy seeds, rosemary, and flaky finishing salt. Set aside.

When the dough is done resting, uncover the bowl and divide the cracker dough evenly into 2 portions. Generously flour your work surface and a rolling pin and roll out the first dough ball. Keep lifting and turning the dough as you roll, to ensure that it doesn't stick to the board and use more flour, as necessary. Once the dough is around ⅛ inch/3 mm thick, loosely wind it around your rolling pin and transfer it to the prepared baking sheet. Unroll the dough from the rolling pin so that it lies flat on the parchment paper.

Brush the rolled cracker dough sparingly with water and top with the seed mixture (you can also just use salt, if you prefer a simpler cracker). Score the cracker dough with the tines of a fork and then use a pizza cutter to slice the dough into 2-inch/5 cm squares or diamonds. There's no need to separate the crackers. Thanks to the score lines, they will break apart easily into individual crackers once cool.

Bake for 8 to 12 minutes, or until the cracker dough is lightly browned. While the first batch bakes, prepare the second similarly.

Crackers always crisp up as they cool, so don't worry if they don't immediately look crisp. They will get there.

Remove the crackers from the oven and allow to cool completely on the baking sheets, then store them in an airtight container. They'll keep for at least 2 weeks at room temperature.

Note: Other really good toppings for these crackers include a dusting of grated Parmesan cheese, freshly ground black pepper, or a thin layer of pesto.

FANCY TOAST

When I first conceived of this book, my working title was *Beyond Toast*. The idea was that most people are familiar with the idea of spreading their homemade preserves on toasted slices of bread, but are at a loss for ideas when they try to push past that classic pairing. My mission was to show people how to move beyond their accustomed notions about where jam and pickles can go and help them put their preserves to work on a far broader continuum. However, for as much as moving beyond basic toast has always been the goal, I think it's also important to include mention of it in a book that's about using preserves.

For me, a good toast experience starts with the bread. I like to choose bread that is interesting, sturdy, and has some flavor of its own. This can be as simple as a sturdy loaf of grocery store multigrain, to an eight-dollar loaf from an artisanal bakery. If you can't find good bread at your local grocery store and you can't swing pricy bread from the fancy baker, try making your own. I've included recipes for Challah (page 118), Oatmeal Sandwich Bread (page 116), and Chutney Loaf (page 123) in this book. They all make truly excellent toast.

Once you've got your bread squared away, let's talk toasting. If you're just making a single slice for yourself, a pop-up toaster or toaster oven is the obvious choice. However, consider upping your game and opting for a griddled slice of bread. I will often heat a cast-iron skillet over medium-high heat, rub my slice of bread with a little olive oil, and lightly fry it in the hot pan. This treatment can transform even middling bread into extraordinary toast.

If you're making toast for a crowd, employ your oven as your toasting device. Preheat the oven to 325°F/163°C. Arrange thick-cut slices of bread on a rimmed baking sheet and brush them with a little tasty oil (olive, walnut, or coconut are all nice). Bake the bread for 7 to 10 minutes, or until the slices are golden and smell wonderful (watch carefully, because the timing varies a great deal depending on the moisture content of the bread). Do make sure that you use chunky slices when employing this technique, so that the centers of the slices remain tender and provide a counterpoint to the crunchy exterior.

Finally, turn your thoughts to toppings. Strive for a balanced slice. For me, that means having a creamy element; a crunchy or textural element; and something sharp, bright, or bitter. Often, one topping can satisfy more than one of these needs. Sauerkraut is a good example of that. It brings both brightness and texture (particularly if it's a relatively young batch).

Finally, here is a handful of ideas for fancy toast. May these serve as a springboard for your toasty imagination.

ALMOND BUTTER AND JAM TOAST

This is the toast of my childhood and something I still eat more than once a week. Toast a slice of grainy, nutty whole-grain bread. While still warm, spread with a roasted almond butter. Top with a slick of berry or stone fruit jam.

RICOTTA AND MARMALADE TOAST

This combination was made Instagram-famous thanks to Los Angeles hipster hot spot Sqirl, but there's a reason why it's caught on. It's an excellent combination. Start with a slice of challah or brioche (you want something rich but sturdy). Toast until just golden and top with a cloud of the best ricotta you can find. Finally, spoon on a generous layer of tart jam or marmalade. If you want to go full Sqirl, apply 2 or 3 flavors in gradient stripes.

AVOCADO AND SAUERKRAUT TOAST

This combination is less traditional that the first two, but it is one of my favorites when I'm trying for a daily dose of fermented food. Sourdough or *pain au levain* is my favorite bread for this combination. Toast a slice until browned and unbending. Mash the flesh of half an avocado into the warm slice and top with a couple of generous forkfuls of crunchy sauer-kraut (this also works nicely with kimchi or *sauerruben* [fermented turnip].

SMOKED OR CURED FISH AND PICKLES TOAST

So many cultures have variations on this theme. You can go Nordic and use cured herring and lightly pickled onions on really sturdy, barely toasted all-rye bread. An East Coast Jewish version involves lox, cream cheese, and half-sour pickles. The of-the-moment foodie version requires a piece of bread made using wild yeast topped with crème fraîche, smoked trout, and pickled ramps. Slightly over the top, but entirely delicious.

DIPS AND SPREADS

A good dip is worth its weight in gold. Good for both parties and easy, speedy lunches, they can get expensive when you buy them exclusively from the store. Happily, the homemade versions are far more affordable and are often quicker than a trip to the market. It does help to have an inexpensive food processor or blender to ease your dip making path, but a handheld mixer can also serve well.

Often, I will improvise a dip by whipping a few tablespoons of whatever chutney is open in the fridge together with a log of goat cheese or a block of cream cheese. I pair this simple concoction with some baguette rounds and call my party appetizer done (a perfectly acceptable approach). For more elevated fare, whip up one of the following recipes!

ROASTED RED PEPPER, PEPPERONCINI, AND FETA DIP

MAKES 5 CUPS/1.25 KG DIP

The bones of this recipe are from a letter published in the July 2003 edition of *Gourmet*. I don't often tear recipes from magazines, but this one spoke to me. I've kept that folded page in my recipe box for more than fifteen years and have made the dip so many times that the original paper is stained and stiff. Presented with an array of cut vegetables and sturdy crackers, it makes good use of the homemade pantry and is a nice staple for parties and open houses.

RECOMMENDED PRESERVES:
I often use my homemade marinated roasted red peppers and pickled jalapeños in this dip, in place of the water-packed peppers and pepperoncini. I also like to use homemade oven-roasted tomatoes in place of the store-bought ones when I have them.

1¼ cups/220 g drained roasted red peppers

1 cup/55 g drained oil-packed sun-dried tomatoes

½ cup/70 g drained and pepperoncini rings (or other pickled hot pepper)

2 garlic cloves

8 ounces/225 g crumbled feta cheese

8 ounces/225 g cream cheese, at room temperature

½ teaspoon freshly ground black pepper

¼ cup/60 ml extra-virgin olive oil (if you prefer, you can also use the oil from the tomatoes)

1 cup/40 g loosely packed fresh basil leaves

1 cup/60 g loosely packed fresh parsley leaves

In the work bowl of a food processor, combine the red peppers, tomatoes, pepperoncini, and garlic and process until well chopped. Add the feta, cream cheese, and black pepper and process until smooth. With the motor running, stream in the olive oil, processing until it is fully incorporated. Finally, add the basil and parsley and pulse until chopped.

Scrape into a bowl or container and chill.

Note: This recipe makes enough dip for a party. Feel free to halve the recipe if you'd like to have a little less.

PRESERVED LEMON HUMMUS

MAKES 4 CUPS/1 KG HUMMUS

One trick I learned from my friend Joy is that the creamiest hummus is made with warm chickpeas (she was the recipe editor for the *Zahav* cookbook and so knows her stuff). The very best way to achieve this is to start with freshly cooked chickpeas (75 minutes in an Instant Pot!). However, if you can't swing that, don't write off this recipe. Instead, tumble the contents of two cans of chickpeas into a saucepan, add a splash of water, and heat them until they're just warmed through.

RECOMMENDED PRESERVES:
You want preserved lemons for this recipe, either home-made or store-bought. If you don't have access to either, try using the zest and juice from one lemon and an extra 1/2 teaspoon of salt.

1 garlic clove

¾ cup/180 ml water

¾ cup/180 ml tahini

2 tablespoons diced preserved lemon

½ teaspoon fine sea salt

½ teaspoon ground cumin

4 cups/800 g warm cooked chickpeas or 2 (15½-ounces/ 439 g) cans chickpeas, drained and warmed (see headnote)

Extra-virgin olive oil, for drizzling

In the work bowl of a food processor, pulse the garlic until minced. Add the water, tahini, preserved lemon, salt, and cumin and process until you have a smooth, creamy, fragrant sauce. Add the chickpeas and process for 5 minutes, scraping down the sides halfway through. Taste and adjust the seasoning as necessary and serve drizzled with olive oil.

Note: Hummus tastes best at room temperature or slightly warmer. Spoon a serving onto a dish an hour or so before eating or zap it in the microwave for 10 to 20 seconds to remove the chill.

BLANK SLATE WHITE BEAN SPREAD

MAKES ABOUT 2 CUPS/500 G SPREAD

Years ago, I wrote a story for an online magazine about white beans. The idea was to offer up a trio of recipes to help our readers use up a pound of beans cooked from scratch. I can't for the life of me recall what the other two recipes were, but this one has stayed with me. I make a batch nearly every week and eat it spread on toast or as a dip for carrot sticks. It's an easy answer to the question, "What's for lunch?"

RECOMMENDED PRESERVES: *I love this spread best with a few spoonfuls of pesto swirled in, but it is also great with chutney, marinated peppers, or the end of a can or jar of harissa. If your addition of choice is a bit watery, you won't need the additional liquid at the end.*

1 (15½-ounce/439 g) can navy or cannellini beans, drained, or 1¾ cups/290 g cooked beans

1 garlic clove, roughly chopped

Grated zest and juice from 1 lemon

1 teaspoon fine sea salt

½ teaspoon freshly ground black pepper

¼ cup/60 ml extra-virgin olive oil

¼ cup/60 ml chutney, pesto, pepper paste, or chopped marinated peppers

1 to 2 tablespoons water (or bean cooking liquid, if you cooked the beans from dried), or as needed

Combine the beans, garlic, lemon zest and juice, salt, and black pepper in the work bowl of a food processor. Pulse the processor 7 or 8 times to begin to break up the beans and garlic. With the motor running, stream in the olive oil. Finally, pulse in chutney. If the spread appears quite thick, add water 1 tablespoon at a time to help loosen it up. Taste and adjust the salt, if necessary.

Note: Truly, think of this dip as your blank slate. I can imagine a version, built on the same bones, made with black beans, limes, and a few tablespoons of really thick homemade salsa. Another easy variation is to add a whole head of roasted garlic along with the marinated peppers. And if you ever find yourself with a surplus of homemade chimichurri sauce, use that in place of the pesto. Delicious!

FROM-SCRATCH QUESO

MAKES 1½ CUPS/375 G QUESO

When I was in middle school, my dad had season tickets for the Portland State Vikings football games. I wasn't particularly interested in college football, but I very much liked going with him for the snacks on offer at the concession stand. My favorite were the "nachos." You got a paper tray with a heap of corn chips from under a heat lamp and a small plastic cup filled with warm, liquid processed cheese. This is my real-food homage to the stadium cheese sauce of my youth.

RECOMMENDED PRESERVES:
Use a tomato-based, chunky salsa here. Avoid uncooked salsas, as they will weep too much liquid into the cheese and can potentially cause the sauce to break.

1 tablespoon unsalted butter

1 tablespoon all-purpose flour

¾ cup/180 ml whole milk

1 cup/120 g grated yellow Cheddar cheese

¼ cup/60 ml drained chunky tomato salsa

½ teaspoon salt

In a small saucepan, melt the butter over medium-high heat. Add the flour and whisk to incorporate. Let the flour mixture cook, whisking regularly, until it has browned slightly and becomes slightly puffy after each round of stirring. Add a small amount of milk and whisk to combine. It will thicken rapidly. Continue to add the milk, whisking to combine, until all the milk is incorporated.

Add the grated cheese and stir until it is melted. Remove from the heat, add the salsa and salt, and stir until just combined. Serve with a bowl of chips or as part of a taco bar.

Note: For parties, I like to double this recipe and put the cheese sauce in a small slow cooker to keep it warm. Place on the buffet alongside a bowl of chips and invite your guests to dip.

Compound Butters

Plain old butter is already one of the hardest-working ingredients in our collective kitchens. It's a spread, a flavor element, and a cooking and baking fat, and it does all that without even breaking a sweat. Why on earth would we ask it to do more? Because it can! In this case, I speak of the delight that is a compound butter. You get all the creamy dreaminess of regular butter, but it's made even more delicious thanks to the addition of jam, marmalade, fresh herbs, and other flavor elements.

Making compound butters with jams, chutneys, marmalades, pickles, and relishes is an easy way to boost the flavor of butter and get your pantry working for you. If you use a vinegar or brine-packed preserve, such as pickles or relish, make sure that you actually squeeze the juice out, as the butter will struggle to hold the liquid. It can also lead the butter to spoil faster.

I like to make compound butters in a stand mixer fitted with a flexible-edged paddle or blade, because that means you don't have to stop and scrape down the walls of the bowl. A regular paddle attachment will also work, but you will want to stop the mixer and scrape the walls several times during mixing. If you don't have a stand mixer, use a hand mixer or get a little upper-body workout and beat the preserve in with a silicone spatula.

BASIC COMPOUND BUTTER

MAKES 1¼ CUPS/300 G COMPOUND BUTTER

8 ounces/225 g unsalted butter, at room temperature

4 to 5 tablespoons jam, marmalade, chutney, relish, or finely diced pickle

½ teaspoon flaky finishing salt

Put the butter in the bowl of a stand mixer fitted with a flexible paddle attachment. Beat on medium speed until the butter is distributed throughout the bowl. Reduce the speed to low and add the preserve 1 tablespoon at a time as the motor runs. Add the salt and increase the speed to medium for a few final seconds.

When the butter and preserve are well integrated, turn off the mixer. Taste and make sure you're happy with the flavor intensity. If not, add a bit more of the preserve. Just take care not to go beyond 6 tablespoons of preserve, because the butter will break if you ask it to hold too much additional product.

Spread a length of plastic wrap on your countertop and scrape the compound butter into the plastic. Form the butter into a log and wrap it tightly. It will keep well in the refrigerator for up to 5 days. For longer storage, place your plastic-wrapped butter in a resealable plastic bag and freeze for up to 6 months.

Below are some tasty variations on this theme.

MARMALADE COMPOUND BUTTER

Add 4 tablespoons of Seville orange or lemon marmalade and ½ teaspoon of flaky finishing salt. Serve with pancakes, biscuits, or scones.

RELISH OR PICKLE COMPOUND BUTTER

Add 4 to 5 tablespoons of well-drained pickle relish or finely chopped pickle and ½ teaspoon of flaky finishing salt. This butter is a really good addition to meat and fish. I occasionally tuck a pat into the middle of a burger when I'm feeling indulgent and I like to roast salmon fillets that are liberally dotted with this butter (using a dill-flavored pickle makes it an even better match for fish).

PRESERVED LEMON COMPOUND BUTTER

Add 3 to 4 tablespoons of diced preserved lemon. No need to add salt here, as preserved lemons are quite salty. This is another butter that is really great with fish, or as a finishing element when you're pan roasting chicken or pork. It manages to be bright, salty, and rich all at once.

SAUCES AND CONDIMENTS

When I was growing up, chicken legs were a staple on my mom's weekly grocery list. They were inexpensive, could be prepped entirely on autopilot, and no matter how much we might grumble at first, in the end we always wound up happily eating them.

She relied on two basic preparations. In the first, she'd stew the chicken legs with canned tomatoes, chopped onions, and whatever seasonal vegetables were at hand (I remember a lot of green peppers and zucchini) and serve it over rice. More frequently, she'd line a baking dish with foil, arrange the legs in an interlocking pattern, and paint them with whatever jam she had open in the fridge. Some nights, the jam was mixed with mustard to make it more savory. Other times, the jam would be stirred together with a splash of soy sauce and spiked with garlic and ginger, for something teriyaki-like. And there were many mornings when she marinated the chicken legs in a slurry of Good Seasons Italian Dressing and runny plum jam, so that all she'd need to do when she got home from work was turn on the oven, slide in the pan, and steam some broccoli.

The beauty of this meal was that while it was essentially the same thing week to week, it didn't feel like that to those of us gathered round the table. That rotating cast of glazes and marinades made those chicken legs seem interesting and fresh, meal after meal after meal.

The goal of this chapter is to help you see your own assortment of jams and condiments like my mom did, as tools to help you vary up your daily cooking while not having to reinvent the wheel every night. You'll find jam transformed into barbecue sauce, simple dipping sauces built from relish or chopped pickle, a quick teriyaki, and my go-to formula for using sweet spreads to enhance a classic vinaigrette. May they become steadfast players in your kitchen, as they are in mine.

HERBED MARMALADE MARINADE

⌒

MAKES 1¼ CUPS/300 ML MARINADE

This recipe is built on the bones of one that Maria and Raphael Baker (the dearest of family friends) once made by the gallon. They used it to dress salads, marinate the veggies, and spread on the sandwiches they sold at the small chain of restaurants they ran for most of the 1980s and '90s. If you lived in Southern California or Portland during those years, you might remember Humphrey Yogurt. I use it mostly as a marinade for chicken thighs and zucchini that are destined for the grill, but it is also a favorite for dressing chopped salads.

RECOMMENDED PRESERVES:
Lemon or orange marmalades work best here, because they convey bitter, sweet, and tart. However, if your preserving habit has led you down the shrub-making path, a couple of tablespoons of this in place of the marmalade is also really good.

⅔ cup/160 ml extra-virgin olive oil

3 tablespoons red wine vinegar

3 tablespoons freshly squeezed lemon juice

2 tablespoons lemon or orange marmalade

2 garlic cloves, minced

1 tablespoon dried basil

1 tablespoon dried oregano

1 tablespoon dried thyme

2 teaspoons dry mustard

1 teaspoon fine sea salt

¼ teaspoon freshly ground black pepper

In a blender, combine the olive oil, vinegar, lemon juice, marmalade, garlic cloves, basil, oregano, thyme, mustard, salt, and pepper. Blend until just incorporated and pour into a mason jar for storage. It will keep in the refrigerator for up to 1 month.

JAMMY MUSTARD MARINADE

**MAKES 1 CUP/240 ML MARINADE,
ENOUGH FOR 2 TO 3 PANS OF CHICKEN**

When my mom made jam and mustard chicken, she didn't do anything more complicated than stir together equal parts jam and brown mustard and spoon it onto the chicken. This one takes that basic idea and elevates it just a touch (though if you're in a hurry to get dinner on the table, there's nothing wrong with her approach).

RECOMMENDED PRESERVES:
I like this best when made with any stone fruit, such as peach, nectarine, or apricot jam. If you have any herb or hot pepper–spiked jams, make sure to experiment with them here.

¼ cup/60 ml jam

2 tablespoons Dijon mustard

2 tablespoons extra-virgin olive oil

1 tablespoon freshly squeezed lemon juice

1 teaspoon fine sea salt

1 teaspoon garlic powder

¼ teaspoon freshly ground black pepper

Stir the jam, mustard, olive oil, lemon juice, salt, garlic powder, and black pepper together in a small bowl until well combined.

Use on chicken, pork, or tofu.

Note: If you have a jar of jam or mustard that's nearly empty, feel free to whisk or shake up this marinade right in the jar. It's a good way to use every drop.

JAMMY BARBECUE SAUCE

∿

MAKES 4 CUPS/960 ML SAUCE

While I often have a few bottles of homemade barbecue sauce in my pantry, I also like knowing that I can take a jar of jam and quickly transform it into something worthy of painting on burgers or grilled chicken. I've also used the sauce this recipe produces as a braising agent for pork roasts; it's awfully good this way (for more on braising, see page 92).

RECOMMENDED PRESERVES:
Choose something fruity and sweet for this sauce. I particularly like jams made from peaches or sweet cherries. Because you're cooking it down a little, this is a good place to use jams that never quite reached their full set.

2 cups/480 ml peach or cherry jam

1 cup/240 ml cider vinegar

1 small yellow onion, finely chopped

2 garlic cloves

¼ cup/60 ml molasses

1 tablespoon dry mustard

1 tablespoon smoked paprika

1 teaspoon fine sea salt

1 teaspoon crushed red pepper flakes

Combine the jam, vinegar, onion, garlic, molasses, mustard, smoked paprika, salt, and red pepper flakes in a 4-quart/3.8 L saucepan.

Bring to a simmer over medium heat. Cook, stirring regularly, until the onion and garlic are soft.

When you're happy with the texture of the onion, remove the pan from the heat and use an immersion blender to purée the sauce into a smooth sauce. If the level of the ingredients is too low to purée well, carefully tip the saucepan so that you have enough depth to allow the immersion blender to do its work.

If the sauce seems too thin for your purposes, cook a bit longer. Remember it will thicken a little as it cools. The sauce is now ready to be used as needed. Any remaining sauce can be funneled into a jar and refrigerated for 2 to 3 weeks.

PLUM TERIYAKI SAUCE

MAKES 2 CUPS/480 ML TERIYAKI SAUCE

When I was young, we had a plum tree in our backyard that produced a ton of fruit every other year. My mom would cook these plums down with minimal sugar into a barely set jam that was best eaten over pancakes or used in this teriyaki sauce.

RECOMMENDED PRESERVES:
Obviously, I like this one best when made with sloshy plum jam. However, it will work with any underset stone fruit jam. I've made it with soft-set nectarine, peach, and cherry as well.

1 cup/240 ml runny plum jam

⅔ cup/180 ml soy sauce

2 tablespoons toasted sesame oil

5 garlic cloves, roughly chopped

2 tablespoons grated fresh ginger

In a blender, combine the jam, soy sauce, sesame oil, garlic, and ginger and blend until smooth.

To use as a marinade, place the protein you're planning on cooking in a resealable plastic bag. Add ½ cup/120 ml of marinade for every 2 pounds/905 g of protein. Squeeze the air out of the bag, seal, and refrigerate for up to 12 hours. If you're marinating animal protein, discard any remaining marinade when you remove the protein from the bag to cook it. Marinades used for tofu and tempeh, however, can also be used as a sauce when the finished protein is served.

To use as a sauce or glaze, it will need to be thickened. Whisk together 1 tablespoon of cornstarch and 1 tablespoon of water. Pour 1 cup/240 ml of the teriyaki into a small saucepan and place over medium heat. Whisk in the cornstarch slurry while the sauce is still lukewarm. Bring to a simmer and cook until it begins to thicken. When it has reached the desired viscosity, remove the pan from the heat.

RELISH AÏOLI

MAKES 1 CUP/240 ML AÏOLI

This is the sauce I call on when I make roasted potatoes or I'm serving steamed artichokes, a childhood favorite. It's a quick thing that uses commercial mayonnaise as its base. I'm always happy when I take the time to stir up this hardworking and delicious combination.

RECOMMENDED PRESERVES:
Acidic relishes and garlicky dill pickles shine here.

¾ cup/180 ml mayonnaise

¼ cup/60 ml well-drained and finely diced relish or pickle

1 garlic clove

1 tablespoon freshly squeezed lemon juice

Fine sea salt

Place the mayonnaise and relish in a small bowl and stir to combine. Using a rasp-style zester, grate the garlic into the bowl. Add the lemon juice and stir. Taste and add more lemon juice and a pinch of salt, as necessary. Cover and refrigerate for at least 30 minutes before serving to allow the garlic to mellow and fully infuse the aïoli.

RUSSIAN DRESSING

MAKES 2 CUPS/480 ML DRESSING

For a large measure of the twentieth century, my family ran a Russian tea room in Philadelphia's theater district. While I don't claim that we're the reason this concoction is known as Russian Dressing, I can tell you that back in the day, this combination of ingredients was the restaurant's house dressing. It was used there on salads, to dress batches of coleslaw, and slathered on sandwiches. Creamy, tangy, and a tiny bit spicy from the horseradish, it's darn good.

RECOMMENDED PRESERVES:
Tangy pickle relish, or finely diced sour pickles

1 cup/240 ml mayonnaise

¼ cup/60 ml ketchup

¼ cup/60 ml pickle relish

¼ cup/60 ml bottled prepared horseradish

1 tablespoon finely minced yellow onion

1 garlic clove, grated or pressed

½ teaspoon fine sea salt

In a small bowl, stir the mayonnaise, ketchup, relish, horseradish, onion, garlic, and salt together until well combined. Leftover dressing will keep for up to 2 weeks in a sealed jar in the refrigerator.

YOGURT TARTAR SAUCE

MAKES 1½ CUPS/360 ML SAUCE

Years ago, I started making tartar sauce as a way to use up an overabundance of relish. Eventually, I resumed making relish because I needed to keep making tartar sauce. It's the perfect accompaniment for the Crab Cakes (page 73) and is excellent served as a dipping sauce for the Pickle-Brined Chicken Tenders (page 108).

RECOMMENDED PRESERVES:
Acidic relishes and garlicky dill pickles are good here, as are finely diced pepperoncini.

- ¾ cup/180 ml full-fat Greek yogurt
- ¼ cup/60 ml finely diced relish or pickle
- 2 tablespoons grated yellow onion
- 1 to 2 tablespoons pickle brine, or to taste
- 1 tablespoon chopped fresh parsley
- ½ teaspoon fine sea salt
- ¼ teaspoon freshly ground black pepper

Stir the yogurt, relish, onion, brine, parsley, salt, and pepper together in a small bowl until well combined. Taste and add additional brine, if needed. Leftover sauce will keep for up to 5 days in a tightly sealed jar in the refrigerator.

HOT BURGER SAUCE

MAKES 1 CUP/240 ML SAUCE

Whether it's made of beef, turkey, or black beans, no burger is served in my house without an offer of this sauce. It hits all the right burger condiment notes: creamy, sweet, tangy, and spicy. And don't be put off by the use of powdered garlic and onion. Most of the time, I use the fresh versions in my cooking, but this one just tastes better to me when made with the dried ones (must be all the McDonald's I ate in high school!).

RECOMMENDED PRESERVES: *Use a savory pickle relish. I like classic, unsweetened hot dog relish, but use what you've got.*

½ cup/120 ml mayonnaise

¼ cup/60 ml ketchup

2 tablespoons pickle relish

1 tablespoon sriracha sauce

2 teaspoons Dijon mustard

1 teaspoon garlic powder

1 teaspoon onion powder

¼ teaspoon fine sea salt

Pinch of cayenne pepper

Stir the mayonnaise, ketchup, relish, sriracha, mustard, garlic powder, onion powder, salt, and cayenne together in a small bowl until well combined. Spread on burgers. Leftover sauce will keep for up to 5 days in a tightly sealed jar in the refrigerator.

JAM VINAIGRETTE

MAKES 1 CUP/240 ML PRESERVES

This vinaigrette is one of my favorite tools for using the last of a jar of jam and is so easy that I feel almost foolish offering a recipe for it. If you want to wing it, use equal parts olive oil and vinegar and just enough jam to bring sweetness, but not so much that it tastes of nothing but fruit. A pinch or two of salt and you're ready to dress greens.

RECOMMENDED PRESERVES:
I like using apricot, plum, or raspberry best, but marma-lades and even fruit syrups can be delicious. If you have a jar of homemade shrub in your fridge that needs using, omit the vinegar and use the shrub to bring both sweetness and acid to the vinaigrette.

⅓ cup/80 ml olive oil

⅓ cup/80 ml cider vinegar

2 tablespoons jam

½ teaspoon fine sea salt

Place the oil, vinegar, jam, and salt in a small jar with a tight-fitting lid and shake to combine. Remove the lid, taste, and adjust the balance of flavors as needed. Use on salads, grain dishes, or even as a garnish for a puréed soup.

PEACH BASIL VINAIGRETTE

Combine ⅓ cup/80 ml of olive oil, ⅓ cup/80 ml of white wine vinegar, 2 tablespoons of peach jam, 2 teaspoons of dried basil, and ½ teaspoon of fine sea salt.

MUSTARDY BLUEBERRY VINAIGRETTE

Combine ⅓ cup/80 ml of olive oil, ⅓ cup/80 ml of cider vinegar, 2 tablespoons of blueberry jam, 1½ teaspoons of Dijon mustard, and ½ teaspoon of fine sea salt.

TOMATO JAM VINAIGRETTE

Combine ⅓ cup/80 ml of olive oil, ⅓ cup/80 ml of red wine vinegar, 2 tablespoons of tomato jam, 1 tablespoon of grated yellow onion, ½ teaspoon of smoked paprika, and ½ teaspoon of fine sea salt.

SALADS AND SIDES

When I was in my early twenties and brand new to Philadelphia, I was invited to join a book club. We met once a month over dinner, rotating among our various houses and apartments. The first time I hosted, I was desperately nervous to cook for my new friends. I made teriyaki-marinated chicken legs, a big green salad, and a warm potato salad that was generously seasoned with chopped dill pickles. The meal was a hit, those dishes are still part of my working repertory, and I'm still friends with a number of the women who shared my food that night.

Home cooks have been using pickles and preserves as reliable flavor boosters for as long as the kitchen has been around. This works particularly well when we're talking salads and side dishes. The handful of recipes in this chapter are the recipes I personally turn to over and over again when I need to feed friends, bring a dish to a party or cookout, or just want to eat something fresh, flavorful, and zippy.

SKILLET-SIZE POTATO PANCAKE

SERVES 4 TO 6

Over the years, I've spent a lot of time frying individual potato pancakes for various Hanukkah celebrations. The end result is delicious, but both you and the stovetop are inevitably covered in a thin sheen of oil by the time the work is done. These days, when I crave a latke, I make this skillet-size potato pancake instead. It uses less oil, requires less attention, and you can easily build a whole meal around it.

RECOMMENDED PRESERVES:
Traditionally, latkes are served with sour cream and applesauce, and you'll never go wrong with this combo. Other good toppings are ricotta and cherry preserves, slices of smoked salmon and slivers of preserved lemon, or a pile of baby greens, dressed with some Tomato Jam Vinaigrette (page 66).

3 large eggs

¼ cup/25 g grated Parmesan cheese

2 tablespoons minced green onion

1 tablespoon fresh chopped dill

1 teaspoon fine sea salt

½ teaspoon freshly ground black pepper

2 pounds/900 g russet potatoes

3 tablespoons extra-virgin olive oil

Preheat the oven to 425°F/218°C.

In a large bowl, whisk together the eggs, Parmesan cheese, green onion, dill, salt, and pepper.

Peel the potatoes and shred them coarsely on a box grater. Place the potatoes in a thin tea towel and twist tightly over the sink to wring out the liquid. The potatoes will start to discolor, but it won't impact the finished pancake. Add the potatoes to the egg mixture and fold together until well combined.

Heat the olive oil in a 12-inch/30 cm ovenproof skillet over medium-high heat. When the oil is shimmering, add the potato mixture. Spread it out so that there is an even layer across the skillet and then use a fork to rough up the top, so it will get brown and crunchy when it's under the broiler.

Cook the pancake on the stovetop for 5 to 6 minutes, or until the bottom is starting to brown and the pancake is beginning to set. Transfer the skillet to the oven and bake for 8 to 10 minutes, or until the potatoes are fork-tender. When the pancake seems cooked through, switch to the broiler setting and broil until the top is golden brown and crunchy, 4 to 5 minutes.

Remove the pancake from the oven and let it cool in the skillet for a few minutes. Once it's no longer piping hot, run a spatula around the sides and under the bottom to loosen, and slide it onto a cutting board. Cut it into wedges, and serve.

QUINOA SALAD with PESTO DRESSING

SERVES 8 TO 10 AS A SIDE

When Scott and I got married, our wedding meal was potluck. Our friends and family brought platters of sandwiches, vast dishes of cut fruit and veg, and more salads than we thought possible. Among those bowls of greens and grains were *four* different quinoa salads. Over time, that number of quinoa salads became shorthand among our family and friends for the kind of wedding we'd had: one that was happy, homemade, and totally appropriate for a girl from Portland, Oregon.

RECOMMENDED PRESERVES: *Every September, I make big batches of pesto with whatever herbs are available, pack them in small jars, and freeze them. If you have a similar freezer stash of pesto, use it here. If not, store-bought is fine, as is a quick fresh pesto made from basil, kale, or parsley.*

2 cups/345 g uncooked quinoa

3 tablespoons extra-virgin olive oil, divided

3 cups/680 ml water

4 ounces/120 ml pesto

¼ cup/60 ml cider or red wine vinegar

Salt and freshly ground pepper

1 red bell pepper, seeded and diced

1 red onion, diced

1 cup/240 ml diced sour pickles

1 (15-ounce/425 g) can chick-peas, drained and rinsed

6 ounces/170 g feta cheese, crumbled

1 bunch flat-leaf parsley, chopped

Pour the quinoa into a fine-mesh sieve or very fine colander and rinse under running water. Heat 1 tablespoon of the olive oil in a medium saucepan over medium-high heat and add the wet quinoa. Cook, stirring continuously, until the quinoa smells toasty and all the water is evaporated. Add the 3 cups/680 ml of fresh water, increase the heat to high, and bring to a boil. Once the water boils, lower the heat to medium-low and cover the pan. Cook for 18 to 20 minutes, or until the quinoa is fluffy and all the water has been absorbed. When the quinoa is finished cooking, spread it out on a rimmed baking sheet so that it will cool quickly and won't become gummy.

In a spouted measuring cup, combine the pesto and vinegar. Whisk the vinegar into the pesto to loosen it. Still whisking, stream in the remaining 2 tablespoons of olive oil. Taste and add salt and black pepper as needed.

Place the red pepper, onion, pickles, chickpeas, feta, and parsley in a large bowl. Add the pesto vinaigrette and stir to combine.

Once the quinoa is cool enough so that it won't immediately wilt the parsley, stir it into the salad. Taste and add salt, if necessary.

Serve at room temperature or chilled.

CRAB CAKES

MAKES 16 SMALL CRAB CAKES

The summer my mom turned seventy, my sister and I coordinated our schedules, brought both our spouses on board, and got everyone to the Oregon coast for a long weekend to celebrate. We rented a house right on the beach, took the kids down to the water every day, and ate lots of ice cream. My dad, sister, and I also snuck away for a morning of crabbing in a rented boat on the bay and caught a baker's dozen of legal Dungeness crabs. The first night, we had a crab feast; and the second, I made these crab cakes. We're still debating which of the two nights was the better meal.

RECOMMENDED PRESERVES: *Make these with a really finely diced dill pickle and serve them with the Yogurt Tartar Sauce (page 64).*

1 pound/454 g cooked crabmeat

3 large eggs, beaten

¾ cup/40 g panko breadcrumbs

3 celery ribs, finely diced

1 small yellow onion, minced

¼ cup/10 g chopped fresh cilantro

3 tablespoons finely chopped pickle (cucumber or green bean are good choices)

¾ teaspoon fine sea salt

¼ teaspoon freshly ground black pepper

2 tablespoons neutral oil, divided

In a large mixing bowl, stir together the crabmeat, eggs, breadcrumbs, celery, onion, cilantro, pickle, salt, and pepper. The mixture won't look like it's going to hold together to form cakes, but it will.

Heat 1 tablespoon of the oil in a large, nonstick skillet over medium-high heat.

Using a 3-tablespoon cookie scoop, filled generously, or a ¼-cup/60 g measuring cup, portion out 8 crab cakes and put them into the pan, spacing them about 1 inch/2.5 cm apart. Cook for 4 to 5 minutes on the first side, using your spatula to gently flatten and shape the cakes. Carefully flip the cakes and cook for 2 to 3 minutes on the second side, or until they are evenly browned and hot all the way through. Repeat with the remaining oil and crab cake mixture.

Serve hot or warm, with Yogurt Tartar Sauce (page 64).

Note: If crab is too dear for your budget, these also work nicely with canned salmon. Use two (15-ounce/425 g) cans, discarding any skin and bones (see Salmon Salad directions, page 74).

SALMON SALAD

SERVES 6 TO 8

This simple salad is the thing I make for dinner when we're running low on more exciting groceries. I try to always have a few cans of salmon in the pantry, and I typically have celery in the fridge and onions in the basket. And I always have pickles. We eat this heaped on salad greens if there are any in the fridge, or even more simply, on toast.

RECOMMENDED PRESERVES:
I particularly love this salad with some chopped pepperoncini in the pickle mix, but just about any sharp, tangy pickle will do.

2 (15-ounce/425 g) cans pink salmon, drained

3 large celery ribs, trimmed and diced

1 small red onion, minced

1 cup/240 ml well-drained and finely chopped pickles

6 tablespoons mayonnaise

1 teaspoon fine sea salt

¼ teaspoon freshly ground black pepper

Tip the contents of one of the drained cans of salmon out onto a plate. Remove any skin and bones and place the salmon meat into a bowl. Repeat with the second can.

Add the celery, onion, pickles, and mayonnaise and stir until well combined. Add the salt and pepper, stir to incorporate, then taste and adjust the seasoning as necessary. I sometimes add a splash of pickle juice if it needs brightening.

This salad will keep for up to 3 days in the fridge.

Note: If you can't deal with the canned salmon that needs to have the fish skin and bones removed, you can buy the smaller cans where the manufacturer has done the work for you. They're more expensive, but are far less bother.

POTATO AND PICKLE SALAD

SERVES 8 TO 10 AS A SIDE

This is my house potato salad and it is a pickle lover's dream. The secret is in how you treat the potatoes before you combine them with the rest of the ingredients. Once they're cooked, you return them to the hot pan and let the heat of the stove steam away the surface water. Then, you add the vinegar to the still-hot pan so that it vaporizes into a fog that the potatoes can absorb. Finally, you dress them with olive oil to seal in the flavor. They're delicious with just a dusting of salt, but when you mix them with the rest of the ingredients, they're downright magical.

RECOMMENDED PRESERVES:
Pickles—whatever you've got. Roughly chopped. The crunchier the better.

2½ pounds/1.1 kg small red or Yukon gold potatoes

2 teaspoons fine sea salt, plus more for potato water

¼ cup/60 ml cider vinegar

3 tablespoons extra-virgin olive oil

½ teaspoon freshly ground black pepper

1½ cups/360 ml well-drained chopped pickles

2 large celery ribs, trimmed and chopped

½ cup/30 g minced fresh flat-leaf parsley

½ cup/25 g minced fresh chives

Rinse the potatoes thoroughly and cut them into bite-size pieces—no need to peel. Place them in a large pot and cover them with water. Salt the water generously, cover the pot, and bring to a boil. Once the pot boils, lower the heat to medium-high and remove the lid. Cook until the potatoes are fork-tender, 15 to 18 minutes.

Drain the potatoes in a colander into the sink and then return them to the hot pot. Return the pot to the stovetop. Let the potatoes steam, uncovered, over low heat for 1 to 2 minutes, then pour in the vinegar. Once all the visible vinegar has evaporated, drizzle with the olive oil and toss the potatoes to coat. Remove the pan from the heat and add the salt and pepper. Add the pickles, celery, parsley, and chives and stir to combine.

Taste the salad and adjust the seasonings as necessary. Sometimes you might need a splash more vinegar, pickle brine, or olive oil.

Serve warm or chilled.

ANTIPASTO PASTA SALAD

∿

SERVES 10 TO 12 AS A SIDE

Forget the bland pasta salads you've eaten in the past. This one is an intense medley of flavorful pickled veg, olives, and feta cheese, with the pasta serving as a welcome break from the sharp, rich flavors. Stir in the feta while the pasta is still slightly warm, which will soften it and add creaminess to the dressing. It's a great one for summer parties and cookouts, because it can handle sitting out unrefrigerated for several hours without spoiling and is actually best at room temperature rather than straight from the fridge.

RECOMMENDED PRESERVES:
I use big jars of homemade mixed pickle (cauliflower, carrot, colorful peppers, and okra) when I make this salad, but if you don't have something like that on your shelf, store-bought giardiniera is the next best thing.

1 pound/450 g short-cut pasta (e.g., penne, fusilli, or cavatappi)

3 cups/420 g chopped mixed pickled vegetables, brine reserved

1 cup/135 g chopped olives (e.g., Kalamata or Nyon)

1 cup/175 g chopped roasted red peppers

⅓ cup/80 ml extra-virgin olive oil

4 ounces/110 g crumbled feta cheese

½ cup/30 g loosely packed fresh flat-leaf parsley leaves, chopped

¼ teaspoon freshly ground black pepper

Cook the pasta in salted water according to the package directions, aiming for an al dente finish. While the pasta cooks, place the chopped pickled vegetables, olives, roasted peppers, and olive oil in a large bowl and stir to combine.

Drain the pasta, shaking it vigorously to remove as much water as possible. Return the hot pasta to the pot and stir in the feta. Let cool for 2 to 3 minutes and then add the pasta and feta to the bowl. Stir to combine. Taste and add the reserved pickle brine as needed. When the pasta is at room temperature and there's no risk that it will wilt on contact, stir in the parsley and black pepper. Taste and add more pickle brine, if necessary.

HOMEMADE PIZZA

MAKES TWO 12-INCH/30 CM PIZZAS

We eat homemade pizza pretty regularly in my house. Sometimes, it is dressed in the traditional manner, with tomato sauce, mozzarella cheese, and cured meat. Other times, I skip the conventional toppings and choose instead to raid my stash of homemade preserves. Jams, chutneys and relishes are all fair game for these pizzalike creations. They're good for dinner, make excellent small bites at parties, and the leftovers are always welcome for lunch.

PIZZA DOUGH

2½ cups/300 g all-purpose flour

1½ cups/180 g whole wheat flour

1 tablespoon granulated sugar

1 (¼-ounce/7 g) packet/
   2¼ teaspoons instant yeast

2 teaspoons fine sea salt

1½ cups/360 ml hot water
   (about 110°F/43°C)

1 tablespoon extra-virgin olive
   oil, plus more for bowl and pans

TOPPING

½ cup/120 ml jam or fruit butter

4 ounces/115 g cheese (choose
   something that complements
   the preserve)

2 handfuls greens

Place the flours, sugar, yeast, and salt in a large bowl and whisk to combine. Add the water and olive oil and work with your hands just until the dough comes together into a ball. Drizzle a bit of olive oil over the dough and smooth over the top.

Cover the bowl with a piece of plastic wrap or a damp kitchen towel and set in a warm, draft-free spot for 1 to 2 hours (the rising time will depend on the room temperature).

Once the dough has doubled in size, gently deflate it and divide into 2 equal-size pieces. At least half an hour before you're ready to make pizza, preheat your oven to 475°F/246°C. If you have a pizza stone or steel, place it in the oven and bring it up to temperature with the oven.

Drizzle a large rimmed baking sheet with olive oil and place one of the dough balls on it. Using damp hands, work out the dough into a flat oval. The secret is to stretch it a little and then let it rest for a minute or two. Eventually, it will relax and stay put. Each dough ball should stretch to mostly cover a baking sheet, with a small margin of bare pan around the edges of the pizza.

Spread half of the jam out evenly across the stretched dough and top with half of the cheese. Place the pan on the preheated stone and bake for

8 to 12 minutes, or until the jam and cheese and are browned and bubbling and the crust is firm. Repeat to assemble and bake the second pizza.

Remove the pizzas from the oven and let cool for 2 to 3 minutes. Top generously with the greens. Cut into slices and eat while still warm.

Note: If you're looking for ideas to use this dough with the contents of your pantry, know you will typically need less jam, jelly, or fruit butter for your pizza than you would if you were using tomato sauce. The idea is to keep these sweet spreads in balance with the other toppings, rather than have them dominate the experience. You'll also see a formula emerge as you read through. I typically pair ½ cup/120 ml of a sweet preserve with 4 to 5 ounces/110 to 140 g of cheese, and finish it off after baking with a generous shower of young salad greens or a flurry of chopped fresh herbs. As you move forward, keep that template in mind and you'll be hard-pressed to go wrong.

PEACH JAM, ONION, AND GOAT CHEESE PIZZA

MAKES ONE 12-INCH/30 CM PIZZA

The summer I turned twenty-six, my friend Roz lived in an apartment that opened onto a cozy, brick patio. At least once a week, our group of friends would gather in this space to cook dinner together on her inherited charcoal grill. Once the main meal was finished, we'd cut two or three peaches in half and set them, flesh-side down, over the cooling coals. Once they were warmed through and nicely charred, we'd eat them topped with small scoops of yogurt, fresh ricotta, or ice cream. This pizza reminds me of those nights.

RECOMMENDED PRESERVES:
Peach jam is best, but any mellow stone fruit jam will work in a pinch.

½ recipe Pizza Dough (page 78)
½ cup/120 ml peach jam
5 ounces/140 g goat cheese
½ red onion, thinly sliced
2 handfuls spring mix salad

Prepare your dough and preheat the oven as described on page 78. Thinly spread the peach jam over the dough. Crumble the goat cheese evenly over the jam. Arrange the thin half-moons of onion on top of the cheese.

Place the pan on the preheated stone and bake for 8 to 12 minutes, or until the cheese bubbles, the jam darkens, the onions frizzle, and the edges of the crust have browned.

Remove the pizza from the oven and let cool for 2 to 3 minutes. Top generously with the spring mix. Cut into slices and eat while still warm.

CONCORD GRAPE BUTTER AND CAMEMBERT PIZZA

∾

MAKES ONE 12-INCH/30 CM PIZZA

This pizza is like a melty, sophisticated version of the cream cheese and jelly sandwiches my mom used to make for me when I was young. Good hot or at room temperature, small squares of this one are great for parties.

RECOMMENDED PRESERVES:
Concord grape butter is the best option, but if you don't have any and can't find any commercially produced versions, low-sugar plum jams and butters will also work well here. Commercial grape jelly is not a good substitute here.

½ recipe Pizza Dough (page 78)

½ cup/120 ml Concord grape butter

4 ounces/115 g Camembert cheese, thinly sliced

2 handfuls baby arugula

Prepare your dough and preheat your oven as described on page 78. Thinly spread the grape butter over the dough. Arrange the slices of cheese evenly over the jam.

Place the pan on the preheated stone and bake for 8 to 12 minutes, or until the cheese bubbles, the jam darkens, and the edges of the crust have browned.

Remove the pizza from the oven and let it cool for 2 to 3 minutes. Top generously with the baby arugula. Cut into slices and eat while still warm.

STRAWBERRY BASIL PIZZA

MAKES ONE 12-INCH/30 CM PIZZA

I was eight years old when I was exposed to the concept of dessert pizza. My family had just moved to Portland, Oregon, and some friends brought a few pies over to our new house to celebrate. Included in the stack was a sweet strawberry-topped pizza, finished with a balsamic reduction and a flurry of chopped mint. I've loved the concept ever since.

RECOMMENDED PRESERVES: *Smooth berry jams are the ticket here.*

½ recipe Pizza Dough (page 78)

½ cup/120 ml strawberry jam

1 cup/170 g diced strawberries

4 ounces/115 g crème fraîche

2 tablespoons thinly sliced fresh basil

Flaky sea salt, for topping

Prepare your dough and preheat the oven as described on page 78. Thinly spread the strawberry jam over the dough. Scatter the diced strawberries on top. Place the pan on the preheated stone and bake for 8 to 12 minutes, or until the jam darkens, the berries soften, and the edges of the crust have browned.

Remove the pizza from the oven and let cool for 2 to 3 minutes. Dollop the crème fraîche evenly over the pizza and distribute the basil confetti over the top. Finish with a pinch of the flaky sea salt. Cut into slices and eat while still warm.

MARMALADE, OLIVE, AND FETA PIZZA

MAKES ONE 12-INCH/30 CM PIZZA

My extended family gets together for dinner once a month. When it's our turn to host, I will often plan a homemade pizza bar. I make several batches of dough and we all make pizzas together. My cousin Sabrina loves bold flavors and this one has become one of her favorites.

RECOMMENDED PRESERVES:
I like this pizza best with classic orange marmalade, but any citrus preserve is good.

½ recipe Pizza Dough (page 78)

½ cup/120 ml Seville orange marmalade

½ red onion, thinly sliced

4 ounces/115 g crumbled feta cheese

2 tablespoons pitted, chopped Kalamata olives

Prepare your dough and preheat the oven as described on page 78. Thinly spread the marmalade over the dough. Arrange the thin half-moons of onion on top of the marmalade. Spread the crumbled feta evenly and follow it with the chopped olives.

Place the pan on the preheated stone and bake for 8 to 12 minutes, or until the cheese bubbles, the jam darkens, the onions frizzle, and the edges of the crust have browned.

Cut into slices and eat while still warm.

Simple Green Salads

I am known in some circles as a salad whisperer. As a result, when dishes are assigned for potlucks and collaborative meals, I am often asked to bring a big green salad. There's no black magic or unique skill involved in my salad construction. Instead, I rely on a simple formula that nearly always leads to success.

It all starts with the salad base. Tender or sturdy, greens are the foundation of a salad and need to be flavorful and in bite-size pieces. Baby arugula is a favorite, but I also often use spring mix, torn red leaf lettuce, shredded cabbage, finely chopped romaine hearts, or young spinach.

Once I know what my starting place is going to be, I pick a collection of toppings, choosing carefully so that there's something crunchy, something creamy, and, if I think the audience will approve, something sweet. Dressings are variations of the vinaigrettes in the Sauces and Condiments section of this book (see page 66).

Here are some of the elements I like to use in salads, and of course, what I use changes seasonally. Your favorite ingredients will likely be different from mine. Consider building your own list so that on nights when you're short on inspiration you can refer to it and be reminded of the things you like.

BASE GREENS

Baby arugula

Butter lettuce (torn)

Cabbage (finely shaved)

Escarole

Kale (stemmed, finely chopped, and massaged with a little olive oil to tenderize)

Red leaf lettuce (torn)

Romaine lettuce (chopped fine)

Spinach (young and tender, please)

Spring mix

Swiss chard (stemmed and cut into ribbons)

SOMETHING CRUNCHY

Celery

Crispy tortilla strips

Cucumbers

Finely chopped pickles (I sometimes also use these as a sweet element)

Homemade croutons (cube bread, toss with olive oil and salt, toast until crisp)

Pickled red onions

Toasted breadcrumbs

Toasted nuts and seeds

SOMETHING CREAMY

Avocado

Blue cheese

Goat cheese

Hummus

Pesto

Queso fresco

Russian dressing

SOMETHING SWEET

Apples (slivered)

Dried fruit (e.g., cherries, cranberries, currants, raisins, or homemade dried grape tomatoes)

Halved grapes

Pickled fruit

Pomegranate seeds (these can also do the work of a crunchy element)

Segmented citrus or canned mandarin oranges

The Basic Salad Technique

SERVES 4 AS A SIDE OR 2 AS A MAIN COURSE

This approach to making salads has never let me down. It works equally well for a lunchtime salad for one as it does for a giant salad scaled to feed 25 at a potluck. Just know that if you're traveling far with this salad, it's best to keep the wet components separated from the greens until just before serving.

3 to 4 cups/75 to 100 g base greens

2 to 4 ounces/55 to 115 g something crunchy

2 to 4 ounces/55 to 115 g something creamy

1 to 4 ounces/30 to 115 g something sweet

1 to 3 tablespoons Jam Vinaigrette (page 66)

Combine the ingredients in a large bowl and toss thoroughly to combine. Dress with vinaigrette as desired and serve.

BABY ARUGULA WITH GOAT CHEESE AND PICKLED ONIONS

SERVES 4 AS A SIDE OR 2 AS A MAIN COURSE

4 cups/100 g baby arugula (roughly chopped if it's leggy)

¼ cup/55 g toasted and chopped almonds

4 ounces/115 g crumbled goat cheese

⅓ cup/55 g well-drained pickled onions

1 to 3 tablespoons Jam Vinaigrette (page 66)

SPRING MIX WITH AVOCADO AND POMEGRANATE SEEDS

SERVES 4 AS A SIDE OR 2 AS A MAIN COURSE

4 cups/100 g spring mix salad

1 cup/110 g homemade croutons

1 avocado, pitted, peeled, and cubed

1 cup/225 g pomegranate seeds

1 to 3 tablespoons Jam Vinaigrette (page 66)

BUTTER LETTUCE WITH WALNUTS AND GOAT CHEESE

SERVES 4 AS A SIDE OR 2 AS A MAIN COURSE

4 cups/220 g torn butter lettuce

¼ cup/30 g walnuts, toasted and chopped

2 ounces/55 g crumbled blue cheese

1 cup/110 g slivered apple

1 to 3 tablespoons Jam Vinaigrette (page 66)

BRAISES, SOUPS, AND ROASTS

Last December, I managed to wow my mom and sister with a jar of salsa, some chicken thighs, and a slow cooker. We were gathered at my sister's house in Austin and it was my turn to make dinner. When you're trying to feed six adults and two picky kids, flexibility and customization is the key to a peaceful mealtime, so I decided to put together a taco bar.

Early in the day, I heaped a couple of packages of boneless, skinless chicken thighs in my sister's slow cooker and covered them with salsa. As the dinner hour approached, I took the lid off the cooker, worked the meat into shreds with a pair of tongs, and increased the heat so that the juices would thicken a little. A few toppings and a stack of fresh corn tortillas later, we gathered around the table and the comfortable quiet of happy eaters fell around us. Later, both my sister and my mom cornered me to ask what I had done to the chicken to make it so good and couldn't quite believe it was just salsa and chicken. They've both made it repeatedly since then. My mom often adds a can of tomatoes, some chopped kale, and a bag of frozen corn and turns it into soup. My sister makes a giant batch and freezes it in resealable plastic sandwich bags for nights when a homemade dinner would otherwise be impossible.

My hope is that this chapter does similar things for your home cooking that the Salsa-Braised Chicken (page 90) did for my own family. And that you look at these recipes and say, "Can something be both so good and so easy?" I think that you'll find that the answer is yes.

SALSA–BRAISED CHICKEN

SERVES 6 TO 8

This chicken is one of my weeknight lifesavers. It is the thing I make when I'm low on both inspiration and time. The first night, I keep the chicken chunky and serve it over brown rice with whatever green vegetable needs to be eaten. The second night, I shred the meat and turn it into tacos. If there's anything left on night three, I add some black beans, sautéed peppers, and frozen corn and call it chicken chili.

RECOMMENDED PRESERVES:
Tomato salsa, salsa verde, and even peach or mango salsa all work beautifully here.

4 pounds/1.8 kg boneless, skinless chicken thighs

2 cups/480 ml salsa

1 teaspoon fine sea salt

Combine the chicken thighs, salsa, and salt in a large, covered saucepan or Dutch oven. Place over medium-high heat and bring to a low simmer. Lower the heat to low and cook until the chicken is quite tender, 45 to 50 minutes.

Remove the lid and cook for an additional 15 to 20 minutes to thicken the liquid, as needed.

Serve over rice, tucked into tortillas, or pull the meat and use it in enchiladas.

Note: This chicken can also be made in a slow cooker or electric pressure cooker. Cook for 5 to 6 hours on low in the slow cooker or for 30 minutes on high pressure with a natural pressure release in the electric pressure cooker. The only downside to these techniques is that they produce a thinner sauce, but you can always reduce it later to thicken.

SWEET-AND-SOUR BEEF SHORT RIBS

SERVES 4 TO 6 WITH SIDES

These short ribs are a great dinner party dish, if you're hosting a gathering of meat eaters. They are best cooked a day ahead and slowly reheated in the braising liquid just before serving. The overnight rest in the fridge allows the flavors to marry and gives you the opportunity to remove the excess fat that will inevitably gather on top. We like them best ladled over polenta and with a side of garlicky sautéed kale.

RECOMMENDED PRESERVES:
Cherry, plum, or nectarine work best here.

2 tablespoons neutral oil

3½ to 4 pounds/1.6 to 1.8 kg boneless beef short ribs

Salt

2 leeks, trimmed, halved, and chopped, and washed well to remove grit

1 large yellow onion, cut into thin half-moons

¾ cup/180 ml water, divided, plus more as needed

2 medium-size carrots, grated

3 garlic cloves, minced

1 teaspoon minced fresh thyme

2 cups/480 ml jam

1 cup/240 ml pomegranate vinegar

Freshly ground black pepper

Preheat the oven to 325°F/163°C.

In a large, oven-safe braising pan or Dutch oven, heat the oil over medium-high heat. Pat the short ribs dry and salt generously. When the oil begins to shimmer, place the short ribs in the pan and brown on all sides. Work in 2 batches if your pot isn't big enough to accommodate the meat in a single layer at once.

When all the ribs are browned, transfer them to a plate and set them aside.

Add the leeks and onion to the pan along with ¼ cup/60 ml of the water. If the aromatics are browning too quickly, add a little more water. Cook, stirring regularly. Any meat or food stuck to the bottom of the pan can be scraped off and incorporated during this stage. Add the carrots, garlic, and thyme and stir to combine.

Add the jam, vinegar, pepper, and the remaining ½ cup/120 ml of water and stir. Nestle the browned short ribs back into the pot, making sure that they're mostly covered with the liquid and veg. Cover the pot and place it in the oven.

Braise the short ribs for 2½ to 3 hours, or until the meat is very tender. When the meat is done, remove the pan from the oven. If the braising liquid has gotten too concentrated during the cooking process, add a bit of water to thin it out. Serve warm.

Note: If you can't find pomegranate vinegar, it's fine to use red or white wine vinegar in its place.

Jam and Vinegar Braises

I almost always have a small stash of imperfect jam in my pantry. These are the jars that have perhaps darkened or faded, or are too firm or never set up at all. They were test batches, attempts at new fruit combinations, or they got lost in my chaotic storage situation and sat just a little too long to be eaten with yogurt or shared with others. They're still entirely edible and perfectly safe; they're just not appealing as is.

I hate throwing the contents of these lesser jars away. Over the years, I have come up with a method for using them that is both easy and makes for some really fine eating. I pull down one of the trusty slow cookers from my collection and put in about 3 pounds of seasoned meat—chicken thighs, pork butt, brisket, or lamb shoulder are all good options. I combine the contents of a half-pint jar of jam with the same amount of vinegar—the variety depends on what I'm making, but I commonly turn to apple cider—and pour it over the meat. If I'm feeling fancy, I'll add some pressed garlic or minced onion, but often I default to a shake of garlic powder and a palmful of dehydrated onion flakes. Then it's just a matter of setting the slow cooker on LOW and allowing it to do its thing for 4 to 8 hours. The cooking times will always vary, depending on the power of your slow cooker, its size, how tough the meat is, and how high the cooker is filled, so be watchful and use your good judgment. You will often find instructions on the Internet about how a Dutch oven in a low oven can be substituted for a slow cooker, but in the case of these recipes, I don't recommend it. In my trials, I found that no matter how low the oven, the jam got too deeply caramelized before the meat was cooked through.

I invite you to take this basic idea and make it your own. For those of you who like more specifics, here are a trio of sure-fire combinations on this theme.

PULLED CHICKEN with APPLE BUTTER AND CIDER VINEGAR

SERVES 4 TO 5

This chicken is good made into sandwiches, stirred into chili, or heaped onto a pile of sautéed cabbage and kale.

3 pounds/1.4 kg boneless, skinless chicken thighs

1 tablespoon onion powder

2 teaspoons garlic powder

1 teaspoon smoked paprika

1 teaspoon fine sea salt

½ teaspoon freshly ground black pepper

1 cup/240 ml apple butter

1 cup/240 ml cider vinegar

Trim away any large bits of fat from the chicken. Stir the onion powder, garlic powder, smoked paprika, salt, and pepper together in a bowl. Layer the chicken and the seasoning mixture in your slow cooker. A 4-quart/3.8 L slow cooker is the perfect size for this recipe.

Spoon the apple butter into a bowl or measuring cup. If your jar is now empty, refill the jar with the vinegar, cap tightly, and shake until all the apple butter bits have come off the walls of the jar. If your jar isn't yet empty, just add the vinegar to the apple butter and whisk to combine. Pour the apple butter slurry over the chicken.

Put a lid on the slow cooker and set it to cook on low. Allow the chicken to cook for at least 4 hours and up to 8.

If the sauce seems too thin for your tastes, remove the lid of the slow cooker and increase the heat to HIGH for 30 minutes. Before serving, use a pair of tongs to work the chicken into shreds.

SPICY PORK SHOULDER WITH TOMATO JAM AND RED WINE VINEGAR

SERVES 8 TO 10

This pork is the perfect centerpiece for a big taco party. Buy a heap of corn tortillas and ask your friends to bring the toppings!

7 to 8 pound/3.2 to 3.6 kg
  pork shoulder

2 cups/480 ml tomato jam

2 cups/480 ml red wine vinegar

3 garlic cloves, minced

1 jalapeño pepper, seeded
  and diced

1 tablespoon fine sea salt

1 teaspoon red pepper flakes

Place the pork shoulder in a slow cooker that holds at least 6 quarts/5.7 L. Spoon the jam into a bowl or measuring cup. If your jar is now empty, refill the jar with the vinegar, cap tightly, and shake until all the bits have come off the walls of the jar. If your jam jar isn't yet empty, pour the vinegar directly in with the jam. Add the garlic, jalapeño, salt, and red pepper flakes and stir. Pour the jam slurry over the pork.

Cover the slow cooker and set it to cook on LOW. Braise the pork for at least 6 hours and up to 12, depending entirely on the toughness of the original cut of pork. Baste the top of the meat if it looks as if it's drying out.

When you're happy with the texture of the pork, use a pair of tongs to remove it from the juices. Let it cool just until you can handle the meat without burning yourself. Remove the big hunks of fat and shred the meat.

At this point, I like to refrigerate the meat and sauce separately, though you can also serve it immediately. If you do make it the day before you want to serve, remove the containers holding the meat and the sauce from the fridge. Remove the fat cap, which is typically quite substantial, from the sauce. Pour the sauce into a pan large enough to eventually hold the meat and purée it with an immersion blender. Bring the sauce to a boil over high heat. Lower the heat to medium-high and continue to cook until the sauce has reduced by about half and is quite thick. Lower the heat to medium-low and return the meat to the sauce. Heat at a very low simmer until the meat is warmed through.

Once everyone has eaten their fill, consider packing up a portion for the freezer.

I never regret having a stash of pulled pork in the deep freeze for those nights when I can't manage to cook from scratch. It also makes a fine addition to homemade chili.

BRISKET WITH CHERRY JAM
<small>AND</small> MALT VINEGAR

SERVES 8 TO 10

It is a bit more trouble to brown the brisket and onions before cooking, but the resulting flavor is well worth the effort. I also love that the finished brisket walks the line between traditional Jewish fare and the smoked barbecue briskets in my sister's adopted city of Austin, Texas.

4 to 5 pounds/1.6 to 2.3 kg beef brisket

Fine sea salt

1 tablespoon neutral oil

2 large onions, peeled, halved, and thinly sliced

1½ cups/360 ml cherry jam

1½ cups/360 ml malt vinegar

Pat the brisket dry with paper towels. Season it generously with salt. Heat the oil in a large sauté pan over high heat. When it shimmers, place the brisket in the pan, fat-side down. Cook for 3 to 4 minutes, or until that side of the brisket has browned nicely. Flip the meat so that the other side can also brown. Once the brisket is browned on all sides, place it in a slow cooker.

Pour the onions into the hot sauté pan and cook for 12 to 15 minutes, stirring often. You want them to brown, soften, and reduce in volume by at least a third.

While the onions cook, pour the jam into a bowl or measuring cup. If the jar is now empty, fill it with the vinegar, cap tightly, and shake until all the cherry jam bits have come off the walls of the jar. If there's still some jam in the jar, add the vinegar directly to the jam in the bowl and whisk to combine. Pour the jam slurry over the beef. Once the onions are nicely cooked, add them to the slow cooker.

Put a lid on the slow cooker and set it to cook on low. Braise the beef for at least 6 hours and up to 8, basting the top of the meat occasionally.

When the meat is quite tender, remove the brisket from the slow cooker, leaving the sauce and onions behind. Place the beef on a large plate or rimmed cutting board and scrape off and discard the gelatinous fat cap.

To serve immediately, cut the brisket across the grain and top with the juices and onions from the slow cooker. For a more refined presentation, leave the meat intact, wrap it in foil, and refrigerate it separately from the sauce.

The next day, remove the containers holding the meat and the sauce from the fridge. Remove any congealed fat from the sauce. Pour in the sauce into a pan large enough to eventually hold the meat and purée it with an immersion blender. Bring the sauce to a boil over high heat. Lower the heat to medium-high and continue to cook until it has reduced by about one third and is quite thick.

While the sauce reduces, cut the brisket into slices of about 1 inch/2.5 cm thick. Once you like the consistency of the sauce, lower the heat to low and nestle the slices of brisket into the sauce. Heat at a very low simmer until the meat is warmed through. This brisket is ridiculously good alongside slices of the Skillet-Size Potato Pancake (page 70).

SAUERKRAUT SOUP

∂᠑

SERVES 6 TO 8

This soup is a great way to make use of really ripe sauerkraut. Perhaps you have a jar that got lost in the back of the fridge, or you simply let a batch ferment a little longer than you normally do. If it's too strong to eat on toast or alongside scrambled eggs, let it work its magic on a pot of soup. I like to eat this in the dead of winter, with a slice or two of toasted sturdy rye bread.

RECOMMENDED PRESERVES: *Simple sauerkraut works best here. If you're using a commercial variety that's packaged in brine, make sure to drain it well before measuring and adding it to the soup.*

8 ounces/225 g thick-cut bacon

1 medium-size yellow onion, diced

2 large carrots, cubed

4 garlic cloves, minced

2 quarts/1.9 L cold water

1 pound/450 g Yukon gold potatoes, cut into 1-inch/2.5 cm cubes

2 cups/480 ml Basic Sauerkraut (page 227)

1½ teaspoons fine sea salt

¼ teaspoon freshly ground black pepper

¼ cup chopped fresh dill (optional)

Place a large soup pot over medium-high heat. Place the bacon strips in the pan and cook until the bacon is quite crisp and has rendered its fat. If your soup pot isn't big enough for all the bacon to cook at once, work in batches. Use tongs to remove the bacon from the pan and let it drain on a paper towel–lined plate. Pour off most of the bacon fat from the pan, leaving about 2 tablespoons behind.

Add the onion and carrots to the pot and cook, stirring regularly, until the onions are browned and the carrots have softened, 7 to 8 minutes. Add garlic and cook until it is just fragrant, 1 to 2 minutes.

Add the water to the soup pot and stir well. Use a flat wooden spatula to work up any bits of browned onion that have stuck to the bottom of the pot.

Finally, add the chopped potatoes to the pot. Place a lid on the pot, lower the heat to medium, and let the soup simmer until the potatoes are tender, 18 to 22 minutes. Once the potatoes are tender, add the sauerkraut, salt, black pepper, and dill, if using, and stir to combine.

Taste the broth and adjust the seasoning as necessary. Serve hot, garnished with the reserved bacon.

PICKLED BEET BORSCHT

❧

SERVES 6 TO 8

Most people assume that beets are the defining element of borscht, but it's actually the bright, acid, near-sour flavor that is the essential qualifier. I've opted for a puréed version here that makes use of a full pint of pickled beets for flavor, color, and texture. Served with a very traditional dollop of sour cream, a bowl makes for a hearty, filling lunch or dinner.

RECOMMENDED PRESERVES:
Pickled beets. Homemade, store-bought, or even quick pickled will work just fine.

1 tablespoon neutral oil

1 medium-size yellow onion, diced

4 garlic cloves, crushed

2½ pounds/1.1 kg beets, peeled and chopped

1 large russet potato, peeled and chopped

2 medium-size carrots, peeled and chopped

2 quarts/1.9 L stock or water

1 pint/480 ml pickled beets, drained, rinsed, and diced, brine reserved

2 tablespoons minced fresh chives

Extra-virgin olive oil, for drizzling

2 teaspoons fine sea salt

Pinch of freshly ground black pepper

Sour cream, for garnish

Heat the oil in a soup pot over medium-high heat. When it shimmers, add the onion. Cook, stirring regularly, for 4 to 5 minutes, or until the onion is fragrant and begins to pick up some color. Add the garlic, beets, potato, carrots, and stock. Stir to combine.

Bring the liquid to a simmer. Once you see it begin to bubble, put a lid on the pot and lower the heat to medium. Cook, covered, for 25 to 30 minutes, or until the beets are tender. They're the densest vegetable in this recipe, so they will take the longest to soften.

While the soup cooks, prepare the garnish. Place the pickled beets in a small bowl with the chives and drizzle them with the olive oil. Stir to integrate.

When the soup vegetables are soft, remove the pot from the heat. Using an immersion blender, carefully purée the soup until smooth. Add ½ cup/120 ml of the reserved pickled beet brine, the salt, and the pepper. Taste and add more salt or pickle brine, as necessary. Don't be shy with the salt; those root vegetables can take a generous amount.

Serve each bowl topped with sour cream and the pickled beet mixture as garnish.

PORK TENDERLOIN WITH CHUTNEY PAN SAUCE

SERVES 4

My mom is Jewish and though she grew up in a secular household, her one point of observance has always been that she does not eat pork. Because she was the primary cook in my childhood home, I grew up rarely eating it myself and had to actively learn how to cook various cuts when I was well into my adult life. This also means that I often forget about things like pork tenderloin, which is a shame, because it is both fast and easy to cook, and pairs up with homemade preserves like a dream. Served with a baking sheet of roasted vegetables, it makes a really lovely, nearly effortless meal. If you don't eat pork, don't ignore this recipe. The very same approach works beautifully for chicken breasts.

RECOMMENDED PRESERVES:
I like this best with chutneys made with apples, pears, or rhubarb. It's also delicious with roughly chopped pickled fruit and homemade mostarda.

1½ pounds/680 g pork tenderloin

Salt

1 tablespoon extra-virgin olive oil

¼ cup/60 ml water

½ cup/120 ml chutney

2 to 3 tablespoons cider vinegar

1 tablespoon salted butter

Pat the tenderloins dry with a paper towel. Season with salt.

In a skillet with a lid, heat the olive oil over medium-high heat until it shimmers. Place the tenderloins in the pan, curling them around each other as necessary. Cook for 3 to 4 minutes on the first side and flip. Continue to cook until the exterior of the tenderloins is nicely browned.

Lower the heat to medium and add the water to the pan. Cover with the lid and cook for an additional 10 to 12 minutes, or until an instant-read thermometer inserted in the middle of the meat reads between 140°F and 145°F/60° and 63°C.

Remove the tenderloins from the pan and set aside on a channeled cutting board or plate. Add the chutney and 2 tablespoons of the vinegar to the pan. Stir with a flat-edged wooden spoon, working up the flavorful bits left in the pan. If the chutney is threatening to get too thick too quickly, add the remaining vinegar. If you still need more liquid, water will do just fine.

Remove the pan from the heat and add the butter. Stir to incorporate. If you want to present this nicely, cut the tenderloins into round slices and arrange them on a serving plate. Spoon the chutney pan sauce carefully over the arranged portions.

APRICOT-GLAZED WHOLE ROAST CHICKEN

SERVES 4 TO 6

I roasted my first whole chicken when I was twenty-one. A senior in college and living in a shabby off-campus house, I had regular access to a kitchen of my own for the first time ever. That first chicken was a puny bird that I managed to first undercook, and then in an attempt to correct that, proceeded to overcook mightily. I've had a bit of practice since then, and over the intervening years, roast chicken has become one of my most comfortable dishes to make by instinct. This whole, glazed version is the thing I make when friends and relatives come over for dinner, because it is both simple to prepare and wonderful to share.

RECOMMENDED PRESERVES:
As the title of the recipe implies, I like to make this chicken with apricot jam. However, most stone fruit jams will work if you don't have apricot. It's particularly good when made with jams you've spiked with herbs or hot peppers.

1 large yellow onion, cut into thick rounds

1 (3½- to 4-pound/1.6 to 1.8 kg) roasting chicken

1 lemon, cut into wedges

1 tablespoon fine sea salt

½ teaspoon freshly ground black pepper

¼ to ½ cup/60 to 120 ml apricot jam, or as needed

Preheat the oven to 450°F/232°C. Arrange the onion rounds on the bottom of a 13 x 9-inch/33 x 23 cm baking dish.

Check the chicken for parcels of necks and gizzards inside and remove them if you find them. Using a sharp paring knife, cut away any large chunks of fat. Pat the chicken dry with a few paper towels and place it on top of the onion rounds. Tuck the lemon wedges inside the chicken. Salt the chicken generously and dust with pepper.

Place the uncovered baking dish in the oven on the middle rack and lower the heat to 400°F/204°C.

Roast the chicken for at least 45 minutes before you begin to glaze it. While it does its initial cooking, measure out ¼ cup/60 ml of apricot jam, saving the rest for later, if needed. Remember, as you brush on the jam, your brush will carry chicken juices back to the remaining jam, and so any jam that doesn't go on the chicken by the end should be discarded.

When it's time to start glazing, remove the chicken from the oven and lower the heat to 350°F/177°C. Using a pastry brush, paint the top and sides of the chicken with the jam. Return the chicken to the oven and continue to roast for another 15 minutes. Remove the chicken and paint on another layer of jam. Put

the chicken back in the oven to roast for another 15 minutes and then pull it out and glaze again.

When another 15 minutes have passed for a total of 1½ hours, pull out the bird again, and using an instant-read thermometer, check the temperature in the thickest part of the thigh. It should read at least 165°F/74°C. The legs should also wiggle in the joints easily and the onions should be caramelized around the edges.

Let the chicken rest for at least 10 minutes before carving. If the onions didn't caramelize to your liking during the roasting process, heat the broiler and place the pan under the direct heat for 4 to 5 minutes, to crisp up those onion edges.

Serve hot.

GLAZED MINI TURKEY MEAT LOAVES

MAKES 8 MINI-LOAVES

Meat loaf always takes longer to cook than I think it should. Every time I make it, Scott and I find ourselves standing in the kitchen staring at the oven, willing it to cook faster. Some might suggest that perhaps I start dinner earlier, but that rarely works. Instead, my solution is to make smaller loaves. They aren't much more work, they're just as delicious, and they cook in about a third of the time.

RECOMMENDED PRESERVES:
These loaves don't absolutely require a glaze, but it's one of those little steps that makes them feel and taste fancier. I like to use tomato jam, some thinned-out pepper jelly, or homemade ketchup to provide that extra polish.

2 tablespoons extra-virgin olive oil

1 large yellow onion, finely diced

4 large garlic cloves, minced or pressed

8 ounces/225 g baby spinach, roughly chopped

Preheat the oven to 400°F/205°C. Line 2 large, rimmed baking sheets with parchment paper.

Heat the olive oil in a medium skillet over high heat. When the oil shimmers, add the onion and garlic and cook for 4 to 5 minutes, or until the onion is tender, starting to brown, and quite fragrant. Add the chopped spinach and the water and cook for an additional 2 to 3 minutes, or until the spinach wilts. Finally, add the parsley, salt, thyme, and pepper. Remove from the heat and allow to cool a little.

In a large bowl, combine the eggs, ricotta, breadcrumbs, and ground turkey. Use your hands to knead the ingredients together. Add the spinach mixture and work it into the meat.

¼ cup/60 ml water

½ cup/30 g chopped fresh
flat-leaf parsley

2 teaspoons fine sea salt

1½ teaspoons fresh thyme

½ teaspoon freshly ground
black pepper

3 large eggs, beaten

1 cup/250 g part-skim ricotta
cheese

1 cup/50 g panko breadcrumbs

2 pounds/900 g lean ground
turkey

3 to 4 tablespoons tomato
jam, homemade ketchup, or
pepper jelly

Divide the mixture into 8 equal-size portions, place them on the prepared baking sheets, and shape them into loaves. Bake for 15 minutes. Remove from the oven and top each loaf with 1 to 2 teaspoons of the jam, taking care to spread it out evenly. Returning the pans to the oven, swapping their positions so that the one that was on the top rack is moved to the lower, and vice versa. Continue to bake for another 10 to 15 minutes, or until the loaves have an internal temperature of at least 165°F/74°C.

Serve hot.

Note: This mixture also makes excellent meatballs. Form into tablespoon-size balls, arrange on the baking sheets, and bake for 12 to 16 minutes. I often make them for potlucks and serve the jam, jelly, or ketchup I might have used as a glaze as a dipping sauce instead.

JAM-LACQUERED CHICKEN WINGS

SERVES 8 TO 10 AS AN APPETIZER

I was much of a wing fan until I tried this approach to cooking and saucing. Using your broiler as the cooking element means you get steady, high heat. This renders the fat quickly, crisps the skin, and in the final stage, causes the jammy sauce to caramelize onto the meat. You wind up with tender wings finished in sweet, tart, slightly spicy perfection.

RECOMMENDED PRESERVES: *Stick with high-sugar varieties of apricot, peach, or cherry for these wings. Stay away from anything that's heavily spiced or includes vanilla.*

3 pounds/1.4 kg chicken wings

½ teaspoon fine sea salt

1 cup/240 ml jam

1 tablespoon freshly squeezed lemon juice

½ teaspoon crushed red pepper flakes

Prepare the chicken wings: If they are still whole, cut each wing into 3 segments: drumette, flat, and tip. You won't want to use the tips for this recipe, but they make really good stock.

Heat your broiler to high and position a rack so that it's 4 to 5 inches/10 to 13 cm away from the element. Line a baking sheet with aluminum foil.

Dry the segmented wings with paper towels and arrange them on the lined baking sheet so that each has a little space around it. Evenly dust the wings with salt. Place under the broiler and broil until the wings are evenly browned and look crisp around the edges, flipping once during broiling. Depending on the strength of your broiler, they will need between 15 and 20 minutes.

While the wings are broiling, combine the jam, lemon juice, and red pepper flakes in a large bowl.

Once the wings are browned and crisp, transfer them to the jam mixture and toss to coat.

Using tongs, return the wings to the pan, leaving the excess jam mixture in the bowl, and broil for 2 to 3 more minutes, or until they sizzle and look satisfyingly sticky.

Remove the wings from the oven and return them to the reserved jam mixture. Toss them again to coat and serve immediately.

Note: If you want wings with a bit more heat, feel free to use more red pepper flakes. Alternatively, swirl a little sriracha sauce into the jam before the initial jam coating.

PICKLE-BRINED CHICKEN TENDERS

SERVES 6 TO 8

Breaded chicken tenders are a perennial favorite with kids and adults alike. Crisp and crunchy on the outside, tender and flavorful on the inside, this version treats the chicken to a quick bath in pickle brine for extra deliciousness.

RECOMMENDED PRESERVES:
I like to use leftover brine from pickled cucumbers and green beans for these tenders. Skip leftover brine from beets, as they will leave the chicken sickly looking and too sweet.

2 pounds/900 g chicken tenders

1 cup/240 ml pickle brine

2 teaspoons fine sea salt, divided

Nonstick spray for rack

½ cup/60 g all-purpose flour

½ teaspoon freshly ground black pepper

3 large eggs

1 tablespoon water

1½ cups/75 g panko bread-crumbs

1 tablespoon Italian seasoning

Note: If your grocery store doesn't sell chicken tenders, you can also buy chicken breasts and cut them into strips, five or six per breast.

Place the chicken tenders in a resealable plastic bag. Add the pickle brine and 1 teaspoon of the salt and let the chicken marinate for 30 minutes to 1 hour.

When you're ready to make the chicken tenders, line a plate with paper towels and arrange the brined tenders on the towels. Blot dry.

Preheat the oven to 375°F/190°C. Place a rack on a rimmed baking sheet and coat the rack with the nonstick spray.

In one bowl, combine the flour, ½ teaspoon of the salt, and the pepper. In second bowl, whisk the eggs with the water. In a third bowl, combine the panko breadcrumbs with the Italian seasoning and remaining ½ teaspoon of the salt. Bread a chicken tender by first dipping it in the flour mixture to coat. Gently shake off the excess. Next, dip it into the beaten egg. Finally, roll the tender in the breadcrumbs, shaking off any excess. Place the breaded chicken tender on the rack and repeat the process with the remaining pieces of chicken.

When all the chicken is coated, bake for 8 to 10 minutes. Remove the pan from the oven and, using tongs, carefully flip the tenders so that both sides can crisp up. Take care to flip gently to make sure the breading stays on the tenders.

Bake for an additional 5 to 6 minutes, or until an instant-read thermometer inserted into the thickest tender reads 165°F/75°C. If the tenders aren't satisfyingly brown, broil them for 1 to 2 minutes at the end of cooking to help them get some color.

Serve warm.

GLAZED HAM

SERVES 12 TO 14

The first time I made a ham, I instantly understood why it's a favorite main dish on many holiday tables. First off, cured hams are already cooked all the way through, so there's no concern about undercooked meat. Second, they're an affordable way to feed a lot of people. And finally, they're delicious. I also like that it's relatively easy to put one's mark on a ham with the addition of a tasty glaze. If you haven't served a big, bone-in ham in a while, I strongly urge you to consider it.

RECOMMENDED PRESERVES:
Apricot is a classic choice, but peach or sour cherry are also good. Another alternative is a whole-fruit lemon jam, should you have a jar or two in the pantry.

1 (6- to 8-pound/2.7 to 3.6 kg) bone-in ham (see note)

1 cup/240 ml water

1 cup/240 ml jam

2 tablespoons spicy brown mustard

2 teaspoons grated fresh ginger

Preheat the oven to 300°F/149°C. Place the ham, cut-side down, in a baking dish. Pour the water into the dish around the base of the ham so that it doesn't dry out. Bake the ham for 1½ to 2½ hours, or until a thermometer inserted toward the center of the ham reads 120°F/49°C.

As you approach that temperature, heat the jam, mustard, and ginger in a small saucepan until the jam is soft enough that you'll be able to paint it on the ham.

Once the ham has reached temperature, remove it from the oven. Increase the oven temperature to 375°F/190°C. Thickly paint the glaze over the exposed surfaces. If all the water around the base of the ham has evaporated, add a splash more. Return the ham to the oven.

Roast the ham for 10 to 15 minutes, or until the glaze bubbles and turns dark brown.

Once the glaze looks good, remove the ham from the oven. Tent with foil to keep warm and let it rest for 5 to 10 minutes before serving.

Note: I've used this technique for both unsliced and spiral-cut hams and it works for either. If you do find yourself working with an uncut ham, make sure to score the exterior with the tip of a knife in a diamond pattern to help crisp it up and give the glaze something to hold on to when it's time to apply. Spiral-cut hams need no such preparation.

KIELBASA, POTATO, AND SAUERKRAUT SKILLET

SERVES 4 TO 6

This is an easy weeknight dinner that I make a lot during the winter. To prevent it from being too heavy, I opt for turkey kielbasa rather than the more traditional pork and I stir in fresh dill at the end of cooking for a burst of fresh flavor. If dill isn't your thing, try chopped flat-leaf parsley or even some roughly chopped spinach. Also note that I don't call for any additional salt in this recipe. This is not a mistake. Between the kraut and the kielbasa, there should be plenty of salt present.

RECOMMENDED PRESERVES:
Any basic kraut works well here. If you ever find yourself with a batch of red cabbage kraut, try making this with sweet potatoes rather than white.

2 tablespoons extra-virgin olive oil

1 yellow onion, halved and sliced

2 large russet potatoes, cut into 1-inch/2.5 cm cubes (about 1½ pounds/680 g)

1 cup/240 ml water

2 cups/480 ml Basic Sauerkraut (page 227), drained

1 pound/450 g kielbasa, diced

⅓ cup/20 g minced fresh dill

½ teaspoon freshly ground black pepper

Heat the oil in a large sauté pan over medium-high heat until it shimmers. Add the onion and cook for 3 to 4 minutes, or until they begin to brown.

Add the potatoes and water. Stir to combine, cover the pan, and lower the heat to medium. Cook for 10 to 12 minutes, or until the potatoes have softened some.

Add the sauerkraut and kielbasa and stir. Cover the pan and cook for an additional 12 to 15 minutes, or until the potatoes are entirely soft and the sausage is plump.

Stir in the fresh dill and black pepper and serve.

BROWN RICE, BEAN, AND SALSA CASSEROLE

SERVES 4 TO 6

This casserole first wandered into my life when one of my college roommates clipped it from our local paper's food section (shout out to the *Walla Walla Union Bulletin*!). We loved it because it was cheap, filling, and designed to be made in the microwave, and we ate it on a near-weekly basis as a result. I use a lot more vegetables these days and finish it in the oven to ensure that the cheese browns nicely, but the essential building blocks—rice, beans, salsa—remain steadfast.

RECOMMENDED PRESERVES:
This is the perfect place for your favorite tomato or tomatillo salsa. Corn salsa is also nice, provided it's tart and not too sweet.

1 tablespoon neutral oil

1 medium-size yellow onion, diced

1 medium-size green, yellow, orange, or red bell pepper, seeded and diced

3 garlic cloves, minced or pressed

2 cups/140 g stemmed and chopped kale

½ cup/120 ml water

2 teaspoons fine sea salt

1 teaspoon chili powder

1 teaspoon ground cumin

2½ cups/500 g cooked brown rice

2 cups/480 ml salsa

1 (15-ounce/439 g) can black or pinto beans, with their liquid

¾ cup/90 g grated Cheddar cheese

Preheat the oven to 350°F/177°C.

Heat the oil in a large, oven-safe skillet over medium-high heat. Add the onion, bell pepper, and garlic and cook for 7 to 10 minutes, or until the vegetables soften and begin to brown. Add the kale and water. Cover and cook for another 3 to 4 minutes, or until the kale has wilted down. Add the salt, chili powder, and cumin and stir to combine.

Add the rice, salsa, and beans and stir. Top the ingredients with the cheese and place the pan into the hot oven. Bake for 8 to 10 minutes, or until the cheese is melted and browned.

Serve immediately.

Note: If you're the type to double recipes and stash some in the deep freeze for a rainy day, allow me to nominate this dish.

YEASTED LOAVES
AND ROLLS

The recipes in this chapter are divided into two categories. The first three recipes are basic loaves that, when sliced, make truly excellent vehicles to transport your homemade preserves from jar to mouth. They are my hardest-working and most versatile loaves that make good sandwiches, excellent toast, and can be dressed up or down as the mood strikes.

The balance of the chapter contains an assortment of leavened loaves and rolls that actually incorporate preserves. There's a babka layered with jam and toasted nuts. There is a loaf that uses a generous scoop of homemade chutney for flavor and moisture. There's a focaccia that can be topped with either sweet or savory preserves. And there's a formula for swirled rolls that can hold all manner of preserves. I highly recommend the version that's filled with Cheddar cheese and chutney.

CINNAMON RAISIN LOAF

୬୨୨

MAKES 1 LOAF

This loaf is a little different from the traditional cinnamon raisin swirl bread we often see at bakeries and grocery stores. Both the cinnamon and the raisins are kneaded into the dough, making for a slice that delivers big flavor in every bite. Next time you have a party, consider baking a loaf, slicing it thinly, and toasting those slices until they're crisp. They are the perfect base for soft cheese, slivers of ham, and dollops of jam.

RECOMMENDED PRESERVES:
*Try it toasted with peanut
butter and pear jam.*

1½ cups/210 g raisins

1 cup/240 ml room-temperature
  water

1½ teaspoons instant yeast

1½ cups/175 g all-purpose flour

3 tablespoons/65 g honey

2 tablespoons neutral oil, plus
  more for bowl

1¼ cups/150 g whole wheat
  flour, plus more for dusting

1 tablespoon ground cinnamon

1 teaspoon fine sea salt

The night before you want to bake, place the raisins, water, yeast, and all-purpose flour in a large bowl to create a sponge. Stir to combine and cover with plastic wrap. Let the sponge rise overnight at room temperature.

The next day, stir the honey and oil into the sponge. In a separate bowl, whisk together the whole wheat flour, cinnamon, and salt, then work it into the sponge by hand to create a dough.

Transfer the dough to a floured board or counter and knead for 2 to 3 minutes, or until the dough comes together into a slightly sticky ball about the size of a large grapefruit.

Drizzle a little oil into the bowl and put the dough ball back in it. Roll it around a little to coat the dough in oil and cover again with plastic to rise.

Let the dough rise until it has nearly doubled in size (because of the raisins, honey, and oil, this bread is a modest riser), 2 to 3 hours. Gently deflate the dough and roll it up so that it's loaf-shaped, then nestle it into an oiled 8 x 4 x 2.5-inch/20 x 10 x 6 cm loaf pan. Cover it with plastic wrap so that the top doesn't dry out and let it rise a second time.

About 45 minutes into the second rise, preheat the oven to 400°F/204°C.

Once the top of the dough crests the top of the pan (this should take about an hour), remove the plastic wrap, cut a shallow channel down the center of the loaf with a sharp knife, and place the pan in the oven. Bake for 20 minutes and then lower the heat to 375°F/190°C. Bake for an additional 30 to 35 minutes.

The bread is done when it has reached an internal temperature of 190°F/88°C. If the top starts to overbrown before the interior has reached the proper temperature, gently cover with a piece of foil. Turn the bread out of the pan and let it cool on a wire rack.

Tightly wrapped, this loaf will keep on the counter for up to 5 days. For longer storage, refrigerate or freeze.

OATMEAL SANDWICH BREAD

MAKES 1 LOAF

This is my favorite sandwich loaf and is one of the recipes in this book designed to serve as a perfect pairing for your homemade preserves. It makes an excellent nut butter and jam sandwich. I also love it under the Rarebit with Relish (page 38) and it's a good candidate for some of the Fancy Toast (pages 41–42). And when it's gotten too dry and crumbly even to be toasted whole, grind it into crumbs, toast them, and use them in place of the panko in the Crab Cakes (page 73).

RECOMMENDED PRESERVES:
This bread can handle just about any preserve you throw at it.

¼ cup/60 ml honey

1½ teaspoons fine sea salt

1 cup/100 g rolled oats

1 tablespoon unsalted butter,
  plus more for bowl and pan

1½ cups/360 ml boiling water

1½ cups/180 g all-purpose flour

1½ cups/165 g whole wheat flour

1½ teaspoons instant yeast

Place the honey, salt, oats, and butter in a large mixing bowl and add the boiling water. Stir to combine and let stand until the oats swell up and the mixture has cooled to lukewarm (110°–115°F/43°–49°C), about 8 minutes.

In a medium bowl, whisk together the flours and yeast. Add that to the oat mixture and stir to combine (use your hands here if you can't hack it with a wooden spoon). Gently turn and knead just a little by hand, until all the flour is incorporated.

Set the dough ball on the countertop, rinse and dry your mixing bowl, and lightly grease it with butter. Return the dough to the bowl and cover it with plastic wrap and a kitchen towel. Set the bowl somewhere warm and let the dough rise until it has doubled in size, 1½ to 2 hours.

Grease an 8 x 4 x 2.5-inch/20 x 10 x 6 cm loaf pan. Gently deflate the dough and roll it up so that it's loaf-shaped, then nestle it into the prepared pan. Cover again with the plastic wrap and let it rise until the dough peeks over the top of the pan by about 1 inch/2.5 cm, 30 to 40 minutes.

While the bread rises, preheat the oven to 425°F/218°C. Remove the plastic wrap, place the pan on the middle rack of the oven, and bake for 10 minutes. Lower the heat to 350°F/180°C and bake until the bottom of the loaf sounds hollow when tapped, an additional 25 to 30 minutes. If you greased your pan well, it should be easy enough to tip the loaf out to check. Just take care to protect your hands. The bread is done when it reaches an internal tem-perature that reads about 190°F/88°C.

Turn the bread out of the pan and let it cool on a wire rack.

Tightly wrapped, this loaf will keep on the counter for up to 5 days. For longer stor-age, refrigerate or freeze.

CHALLAH

MAKES 1 LOAF

I started baking with my Great-Aunt Doris when I was five years old. She'd wrap me up in an apron, I'd climb onto a kitchen chair positioned next to the counter, and she'd spin stories of when she and my grandmother were little girls in with the flour and butter. We started with cinnamon twists, moved on to Quick Strudel (page145), and finally, when she thought I was ready for yeast, we moved on to challah. Aunt Doris didn't dwell on the religious significance of the traditional loaf (though I now know it is steeped in history). She simply stated that every Jewish woman needed to know how to make challah. I cannot bake a loaf without thinking of her.

RECOMMENDED PRESERVES:
This bread is the perfect vehicle for any sweet spread and also is terrific in the Layered Bread Pudding (page 168).

3 tablespoons honey

1 cup/240 ml warm water (110°F/43°C)

2 teaspoons active dry yeast

4½ cups/540 g all-purpose flour, divided

1½ teaspoons fine sea salt

2 large eggs, beaten

1 large egg, separated

¼ cup/60 ml neutral oil, plus more for bowl

Stir the honey into the warm water until it begins to dissolve. Sprinkle the yeast across the top of the water and let it sit for 10 minutes, or until the yeast is frothy.

Place 4 cups/480 g of the flour in the bowl of a stand mixer fitted with the paddle attachment (you can also mix this by hand, but using a mixer is admittedly easier). Stir in the salt. Add the beaten eggs, extra egg yolk, oil, and the yeast mixture. Mix to combine. Once the ingredients are integrated, switch to the dough hook and begin to knead (you can also do this by hand on a board).

Work the dough for 5 to 7 minutes, adding more flour to the dough as you work, if it's too sticky to knead effectively. Eventually, the dough should come together into a soft, slightly tacky, smooth ball.

Grease a large bowl with a drizzle of oil and place the dough ball in the bowl. Move it around until the dough is fully coated with the oil. Cover with a plastic bag, plastic wrap, or a damp kitchen towel and tuck it some place warm for a couple hours, or until the dough has doubled in size.

Once the dough has risen sufficiently, gently deflate it. Divide the dough into 6 portions and roll them out into thin ropes about 14 to 16 inches/35 to 45 cm in length. Initially they won't want to maintain their length, but if you let them rest a little between each stretch-and-roll session, they will eventually relax into the shape.

When all your strands are of the appropriate length, lay them out next to one another. Gather them together at the top and give them a good pinch to secure them together. Then, begin your braid.

Starting on the right side, grab the strand that is next to the farthest to the right and cross it over to the far left. Then, grab the farther right strand and move it to the middle of the strands. Shifting to the left side of the strands, pick up the strand that is one in from the far left and move it all the way over to the far right. Then pick up the farthest left strand and move it to the middle.

Continue like this, alternating sides, moving the second strand from the edge over to the other side of the loaf and then moving the farthest strand to the middle, until you've braided the whole loaf. Pinch the braided ends together and tuck under the loaf a bit.

Once your braid is complete, place it on a parchment-lined baking sheet and cover it with plastic wrap while it rises for about an hour, or until the strands look plump. As the loaf rises, preheat the oven to 350°F/177°C. When the loaf has finished rising, whisk the reserved egg white together with a tablespoon of water. Using a pastry brush, generously paint the loaf with the egg wash.

Bake the challah for 30 to 35 minutes. It is done when it is deeply browned and sounds hollow when you tap the bottom. If you have an instant-read thermometer, the interior of the loaf should register 190°F/88°C.

Let the loaf cool completely on a wire rack before slicing.

BABKA

MAKES 2 LOAVES

Some people think a babka requires chocolate to truly be called a babka, but I firmly believe that jam makes just as good a filling. I use a trick here that I learned from fellow canning author Cathy Barrow and add some freshly made breadcrumbs (see note) to the filling to help hold the jam and nuts in place.

RECOMMENDED PRESERVES:
Opt for something sweet and well set here. I like apricot, cherry, or peach jam, but seedless raspberry would also be good.

1 cup/240 ml milk

2 tablespoons/25 g active dry yeast

4 cups/480 g all-purpose flour, plus more for dusting

1 teaspoon fine sea salt

6 tablespoons/85 g unsalted butter, at room temperature, plus more for bowl and pans

½ cup/100 g granulated sugar

2 large eggs

1 teaspoon vanilla extract

6 tablespoons/85 g melted unsalted butter

2 cups/480 ml jam (each cup can be a different flavor, as they won't mix)

2 cups/240 g walnuts or pecans, toasted and chopped

1 cup/40 g fresh breadcrumbs (see note)

1 large egg, beaten with a little water

Heat the milk in a small pot over low heat or in a glass measuring cup in the microwave just until lukewarm (110°–120°F/43°–49°C). Sprinkle the yeast on top of the warm milk and let it sit for 5 minutes, or until it is foamy.

Whisk the flour and salt together in a large bowl.

Combine the room-temperature butter and sugar in the bowl of a stand mixer fitted with a paddle attachment and beat until light and fluffy. Add the eggs and vanilla and mix until well integrated. With the mixer running on low speed, alternate between adding the flour mixture and the milk, until both are incorporated.

Stop the mixer and switch to the dough hook. Knead for 4 to 6 minutes on low speed, or until the dough comes together and seems quite soft and smooth.

Butter a large bowl and set the dough in it. Cover with plastic wrap and set the bowl in a warm spot to rise until the dough has doubled (remember that if your ingredients were quite chilly, the rising time might be even longer), between 1 and 2 hours.

Once the dough has doubled, gently deflate it. At this point, you can either refrigerate your dough and pick up the following day, or you can proceed. If you do put the dough in the fridge overnight, you will need to give it a couple of hours at room temperature to warm up before proceeding.

Divide the dough into 2 equal-size portions. Dust your work surface with flour and roll out the first portion of dough into an 18 x 12-inch/46 x 30 cm rectangle. Leaving a 1-inch/2.5 cm border of bare dough on one of the short edges, generously paint the dough with half of the melted butter. Spread 1 cup/240 ml of the jam over the butter. Distribute half of the toasted nuts and half the breadcrumbs over the jam.

Starting with the short edge without the uncovered 1-inch/2.5 cm border, carefully roll the dough into a tight log, working toward the bare edge.

Once the dough is rolled, press it down to seal. Slice the loaf in half lengthwise down the middle, leaving the top inch/2.5 cm of the roll uncut and still intact.

To twist the babka into its traditional shape, grab the ends and twist them in opposite directions toward the outsides of the loaf. Some of the nuts will fall out as you do this and the loaf might look a little funny. The second rise should resolve any issues.

Repeat the rolling, filling, rolling, and twisting with the second batch of dough.

Nestle the twisted loaves into buttered loaf pans, cover them with plastic wrap, and let them rise for about an hour at room temperature, or until they puff and begin to approach the rim of the baking pans. While they rise, preheat the oven to 350°F/177°C. Brush the babka with the egg wash and bake until an instant-read thermometer indicates that the loaf is about 190°F/88°C inside, 35 to 40 minutes. Make sure to test the temperature for both loaves, just in case your dough was imperfectly divided.

If the jam begins to caramelize excessively before the internal temperature rises to the proper point, cover the loaves with aluminum foil and continue to bake.

Remove the pans from the oven, set them on a wire rack, and allow the loaves to cool until the jam is no longer molten and the layers have started to meld together. When you're safely able to handle the loaves, remove them from the pans and let them cool to room temperature on the racks.

Note: Making fresh breadcrumbs couldn't be easier. Simply pulse stale or lightly toasted bread in a food processor. You can save scraps of good bread in the freezer for this purpose.

CHUTNEY LOAF

MAKES 1 LOAF

The idea for this loaf came from UK food writer Dan Lepard. In his baking book *Short and Sweet,* he includes a recipe for a Winter Apple Loaf that includes a generous portion of chopped apple, minced onion, and hard cider or vinegar. That combination of ingredients is similar to how many of my favorite chutneys start, and I began to wonder whether I could bake a sliceable loaf that included a healthy portion of chutney in the dough. This recipe is the result of that moment of curiosity and I could not be happier with the outcome.

RECOMMENDED PRESERVES:
Chutneys made with apples, pears, peaches, or apricots work best. Avoid uncooked chutneys, as they don't work as well.

½ cup/120 ml chutney

1 cup/240 ml warm water (around 100°F/38°C)

2¼ teaspoons instant yeast

3½ cups/420 g all-purpose flour, plus more for dusting

¾ cup/110 g toasted sunflower seeds

1½ teaspoons fine sea salt

Oil for bowl and pan

Place the chutney, water, and yeast in a large mixing bowl. Stir to combine. Add the flour, sunflower seeds, and salt. Stir with a wooden spoon until the dough starts to come together and then switch to using your hands. Work the dough in the bowl until all the flour is incorporated. Form the sticky dough into a ball and drizzle a little oil on top. Rub the oil across the top of the dough and around the sides of the bowl. Cover with plastic wrap or a damp kitchen towel and let rise until it has nearly doubled in bulk, 1½ to 2 hours. Grease an 8 x 4 x 2.5-inch/20 x 10 x 6 cm loaf pan.

Gently deflate the dough and roll it up so that it's loaf-shaped, then nestle it into the prepared pan. Cover again with the plastic wrap and let it rise until the dough just peeks over the top of the pan, 30 to 40 minutes.

While the dough rises, preheat the oven to 425°F/218°C. Remove the plastic wrap, place the pan on the middle rack of the oven, and bake for 10 minutes. Then, lower the heat to 350°F/180°C and bake until the bottom of the loaf sounds hollow when tapped, an additional 25 to 30 minutes (if you greased your pan well, it should be easy to tip the loaf out to check). The bread is done when it reaches an internal temperature that reads about 190°F/88°C.

Turn bread out of the pan and let it cool on a wire rack.

Tightly wrapped, this loaf will keep on the counter for up to 5 days. For longer storage, refrigerate or freeze.

FOCACCIA WITH PRESERVES

MAKES 1 LARGE FOCACCIA

Anyone who has done any home canning should have focaccia in their recipe file. It is easy to make, is incredibly flexible, and takes to nearly any preserve you heap on top. Whether you need something to take to a friend's house or you just want a tasty batch of bread to serve with a pot of soup, this recipe can adapt to suit your needs.

RECOMMENDED PRESERVES:
Any not-too-sweet jam, chutney, or relish will work here. If you're going in a savory direction, consider scattering some slivered onions or a handful of chopped fresh herbs on top of your preserve.

5 cups/600 g all-purpose flour, plus more for dusting

2 tablespoons granulated sugar

1 tablespoon fine sea salt

2¼ teaspoons instant yeast

1¾ cups/420 ml warm water (110°–115°F/43°–48°C)

3 tablespoons olive oil, divided

1 cup/240 ml jam, chutney, or relish

Flaky finishing salt, for sprinkling

In the bowl of a stand mixer fitted with a paddle attachment, stir together the flour, sugar, salt, and yeast. Add the water and mix to combine. Once the water is integrated, switch to the dough hook and knead until the dough is stretchy, 4 to 5 minutes.

Remove the bowl from the mixer. Wet your hands and coax the dough into a ball. Coat it with a tablespoon of oil. Cover the bowl with a damp towel and let the dough rise until it has doubled in size, about an hour or so. Gently deflate the dough and fold it over itself a few times. Reshape it into a smooth ball and let it double in size a second time (this can be done overnight in the refrigerator. If you choose this route, let the dough return to room temperature for about 2 hours before proceeding with baking).

While the dough rises a second time, preheat the oven to 425°F/218°C. Grease an 18 x 13-inch/46 x 33 cm rimmed baking sheet with the remaining 2 tablespoons of oil. Once the dough is finished its second rise, turn it out onto the prepared pan. Using your hands, stretch it out to the corners of the pan, making small holes with your fingertips as you stretch the dough. The holes will close during baking, but if you don't make holes through to the bottom of the pan, the bread won't have its characteristic craggy, pockmarked surface. If the dough is bouncing back too much, let it rest a few minutes and resume your stretching and prodding.

Spread the focaccia dough with the jam. If you're using a really strongly flavored preserve to top this focaccia, consider using a bit less than the full cup suggested in the ingredients. You can always add more, but it's hard to back off once the bread is finished.

Sprinkle with the flaky finishing salt. Let it rise again for 10 minutes.

Bake until the top is nicely burnished and a peek at the bottom shows an even brown exterior, 22 to 25 minutes. Remove from the oven and let the focaccia cool in the pan. Do let it cool to room temperature before slicing, to prevent it from becoming gummy inside.

Note: For a thicker, doughier focaccia, bake in a 13 x 9 inch/33 x 23 cm pan. Just make sure to really increase the baking time by at least 5 minutes to ensure that the focaccia is fully baked.

SWIRLED ROLLS

MAKES 12 ROLLS

These swirled rolls look like cinnamon rolls but have a whole lot more going on in the flavor department. Because the dough is barely sweetened, it is highly flexible and can be filled with either sweet or savory spreads. The dough recipe makes enough for 12 rolls, so if you want some sweet and some savory from a single batch, divide the dough in two, fill as you desire, and divide the finished rolls between a pair of pie plates.

RECOMMENDED PRESERVES: *Any well set jam will work here. Apple and pumpkin butter are also delicious.*

DOUGH

3 cups/360 g all-purpose flour, plus more for dusting

2 tablespoons granulated sugar

2¼ teaspoons instant yeast

1 teaspoon fine sea salt

½ cup/120 ml whole milk

½ cup/120 ml water

1 large egg yolk

Place the flour, sugar, instant yeast, and salt in the bowl of a stand mixer fitted with the paddle attachment. Stir to combine.

In a spouted measuring cup, whisk together the milk, water, and the egg yolk.

With the mixer running on low speed, stream in the melted butter. Once it is fully incorporated, do the same with the milk mixture.

Once the liquids are fully incorporated, stop the mixer and switch to the dough hook and knead on medium speed for 3 to 4 minutes, or until the dough looks quite elastic.

Grease a large mixing bowl with the room-temperature butter. Working with damp hands to keep the dough

4 tablespoons/55 g unsalted
butter, melted

1 tablespoon unsalted butter,
at room temperature

FILLING

1 tablespoon unsalted butter,
at room temperature

1½ cups/360 ml jam

2 cups/300 g raisins

from sticking to you, roughly shape the dough into a
ball and tuck it into the prepared bowl. Cover the bowl
with plastic wrap or a damp kitchen towel and let it rise
until the dough has roughly doubled, 1½ to 2 hours.

Butter a 13 x 9-inch/33 x 23 cm baking dish. Dust
your work surface with flour and place the dough on
the floury spot. Gently deflate the dough while push-
ing it into a rough rectangle.

Using a floured rolling pin, coax the dough into a 20
x 12-inch/50 x 30 cm rectangle. Pour the jam onto the
dough and, using an offset spatula, spread it out to cover
the dough, leaving a 1-inch/2.5 cm border of bare dough
on the long edge farthest from you. Evenly distribute
the raisins on top of the jam. Starting at the edge closest
to you, begin to roll the dough toward the bare border.
Wrap as tightly as you can without tearing the dough.

When you've reached the border of dough, dab it
with water and roll to close. Position the dough log
so that the seam is on the bottom. Using a serrated
knife, cut the dough into 12 rolls about 1½ inches/4 cm
in thick. The easiest way to do this is to cut the log in
half first, then each half in half. Then, cut each of the 4
portions into 3. It's easier to manage and eyeball when
you're working with smaller segments.

Arrange the rolls in the buttered baking dish so that they
aren't touching and the spirals face up. Cover the rolls with
plastic wrap or a damp kitchen towel and let them rise until
they've grown to touch one another, about an hour.

Ten to 15 minutes before you want to bake, preheat
the oven to 350°F/177°C. When the rolls are fully
risen, uncover and place the baking dish in the hot
oven. Bake for 35 to 40 minutes, or until the rolls are
golden on top and an instant-read thermometer reads
at least 200°F/93°C when inserted into the middle of
the center roll.

Remove the pan from the oven and let the rolls cool
in the baking dish.

FILLED SWEET ROLLS

MAKES 12 ROLLS

These tasty rolls are filled with the jam, jelly, marmalade, or fruit butter of your choice. Most recently, I made a batch with Concord grape butter and a scattering of toasted peanuts in place of the raisins written into the recipe.

RECOMMENDED PRESERVES:
Any sweet spread will work well here.

1 tablespoon unsalted butter, softened

1 recipe Swirled Rolls dough (page 126), rolled and ready to fill

1½ cups/360 ml jam

2 cups/300 g golden raisins (these are optional if you hate them)

GLAZE

2 cups/227 g confectioners' sugar

1 teaspoon vanilla extract

2 to 4 tablespoons/30 to 60 ml milk, or as needed

Butter a 13 x 9-inch/33 x 23 cm baking dish. Roll out the dough as described on page 126. Pour the jam onto the dough and, using an offset spatula, spread it out to cover the dough, leaving a 1-inch/2.5 cm border of bare dough on the long edge farthest from you. Evenly distribute the raisins on top of the jam. Starting at the edge closest to you, begin to roll the dough toward the bare border. Wrap as tightly as you can without tearing the dough.

When you've reached the unfilled edge of dough, dab it with water and roll to close. Position the dough log so that the seam is on the bottom. Using a serrated knife, cut the dough into 12 rolls about 1½ inches/4 cm thick. The easiest way to do this is to cut the log in half first, then each half in half. Then, cut each of the 4 portions into 3. It's easier to manage and eyeball when you're working with smaller segments.

Arrange the rolls in the buttered baking dish so that they aren't touching and the spirals face up. Cover the rolls with plastic wrap or a damp kitchen towel and let them rise until they've grown to touch one another, about an hour.

Ten to 15 minutes before you want to bake, preheat the oven to 350°F/177°C. When the rolls are fully risen, uncover and place the baking dish in the hot oven. Bake for 35 to 40 minutes, or until they are golden on top and an instant-read thermometer reads at least 200°F/93°C when inserted into the middle of the center roll.

Remove the pan from the oven and let the rolls cool in the baking dish.

Prepare the glaze: In a medium bowl, stir together the confectioners' sugar, vanilla, and 2 tablespoons of milk with a fork or whisk, pressing out any lumps. If it seems too think to pour, add additional milk a splash at a time.

Once the rolls are nearly room temperature, drizzle the glaze across the top.

CHEESE AND CHUTNEY ROLLS

MAKES 12 ROLLS

The idea of a savory rolled bun, filled with cheese and chutney, lived in my head long before I made them. I'm happy to say that they are even better in reality than they were in my imagination. The dough is tender and the cheese and chutney meld during baking to become a higher version of their individual selves. They elevate a bowl of soup and are a fun addition to a brunch gathering.

RECOMMENDED PRESERVES: *The most important thing to do when tackling this recipe is to make sure that the pairing of cheese and chutney is harmonious. If they go well together, everything else will fall into place.*

3 tablespoons unsalted butter, at room temperature, divided

1 recipe Swirled Rolls dough (page 126), rolled and ready to fill

1½ cups/360 ml apple or pear chutney

2 cups/240 g grated Cheddar cheese

Butter a 13 x 9-inch/33 x 23 cm baking dish with 1 tablespoon of the butter. Roll out the dough as described on page 126. Pour the chutney onto the dough and, using an offset spatula, spread it out to cover the dough, leaving a 1-inch/2.5 cm border on the long edge furthest from you. Distribute the cheese evenly across the chutney-covered territory. Starting at the edge closest to you, begin to roll the dough toward the border. Wrap as tightly as you can without tearing the dough.

When you've reached the outer edge, dab the dough with water and roll to close. Position the dough log so that the seam is on the bottom so that it stays closed during slicing. Using a serrated knife, cut the dough into 12 rolls about 1½ inches/4 cm thick. The easiest way to do this is to cut the log in half first, then each half in half. Then, cut each of the 4 portions into 3. It's easier to manage and eyeball when you're working with smaller segments.

Arrange the rolls in the buttered baking dish so that they aren't touching and the spirals face up. Cover the rolls with plastic wrap or a damp kitchen towel and let them rise until they've grown to touch one another, about an hour.

Ten to 15 minutes before you want to bake, preheat the oven to 350°F/177°C. When the rolls are fully risen, uncover and place the baking dish in the hot oven. Bake for 35 to 40 minutes, or until they are golden on top, the cheese is melted, and an instant-read thermometer reads at least 200°F/93°C when inserted into the middle of the center roll.

Remove the baking dish from the oven. Rub the remaining 2 tablespoons of butter over the tops of the hot rolls. Serve warm.

COOKIES AND BARS

When most people think of incorporating jam into a cookie, the first thing that springs to mind is the classic thumbprint cookie. Traditionally made with tender, butter-rich dough and finished with a pool of sweet jam, it is an outstanding cookie. However, the jammy cookie train doesn't stop there. I like to stir jam into billowy meringue cookies, spread it out into bars, fold it into triangular Hamantaschen, and roll it into sliceable cookies. You can spread it into rugelach dough or make a savory blue cheese shortbread to serve at a cocktail party. What all these cookies have in common is that they use a consequential amount of jam, are relatively easy to make, and are downright delicious. What are you waiting for? It's time to start baking!

CLASSIC BUTTERY THUMBPRINTS

MAKES 4 DOZEN COOKIES

In search of a rich, buttery, classic thumbprint cookie? Look no further than this recipe. It is quick, can be made with kids, and never fails to delight. It also uses a dough that does not need to be chilled before baking, which means you can go from craving to cookie in less than an hour.

RECOMMENDED PRESERVES:
I like chunky jams in my thumbprints, because they give added interest and texture to a simple cookie. Whatever you choose, opt for something with a strong set, as really syrupy jams often dribble out of the cookie during baking.

1 cup/225 g unsalted butter, at room temperature

⅔ cup/135 g granulated sugar

2 large egg yolks

1 teaspoon vanilla extract

2 cups/240 g all-purpose flour

½ teaspoon fine sea salt

Preheat the oven to 350°F/177°C. Line a pair of rimmed baking sheets with parchment paper or silicone baking mats.

In a stand mixer fitted with a paddle attachment, cream the butter and sugar together. Add the egg yolks and vanilla and beat until combined.

Place the flour and salt in a medium mixing bowl and whisk to combine. Add the flour mixture to the mixer bowl and run on low speed, just until the dough comes together.

Using a 1-tablespoon cookie scoop or a pair of soup spoons, portion the dough into balls of about 1 tablespoon each. Roll the portioned dough into smooth balls, arrange them on the prepared baking pans (I find that 12 cookies per sheet works best), and press a hollow into the center of each cookie with your thumb. Dip your thumb into a dish of water every third or fourth cookie, to keep the dough from sticking.

Dollop about ½ teaspoon of jam into each cookie. Bake for 12 to 15 minutes, or until the cookies are just barely browned. Let the cookies cool on the baking sheets for 2 to 3 minutes, just until they have enough structure to be carefully moved to a wire rack. Repeat the process with the remaining dough.

Once baked, these cookies will keep for 3 to 4 days at room temperature in an airtight container. For longer-term storage, wrap well and freeze.

PEANUT BUTTER *AND* OATMEAL THUMBPRINTS

MAKES 3 TO 4 DOZEN COOKIES

These cookies marry the best of a peanut butter cookie with the hearty goodness of an oatmeal cookie and then finish it off with a tasty pool of jam. While I love the classic version of the thumbprint cookie, this one is a close second in my heart. For those who need to avoid peanuts due to allergies, I've made this same cookie with sunflower seed butter with delicious, if slightly more crumbly, results.

RECOMMENDED PRESERVES:
This cookie works best with something that's on the more firmly set end of the spectrum. If all you've got is runny jam, try cooking it down in a small saucepan before spooning it into the center of the cookie. These cookies are also a great way to finish off open jars, so survey the fridge before opening something fresh.

1 cup/260 ml smooth natural peanut butter

½ cup/110 g packed light brown sugar

¼ cup/60 g unsalted butter, at room temperature

¼ cup/60 ml applesauce

1 large egg

1 teaspoon vanilla extract

1 cup/120 g all-purpose flour

1 cup/90 g quick-cooking oats (or give your rolled oats a quick blitz in the blender)

½ teaspoon fine sea salt

½ teaspoon baking powder

1 cup/240 ml jam

Preheat the oven to 350°F/177°C. Line 2 rimmed baking sheets with parchment paper or silicone baking mats.

In the bowl of a stand mixer fitted with the paddle attachment, mix the peanut butter, brown sugar, butter, and applesauce together. Once combined, add the egg and vanilla and beat to incorporate.

In medium bowl, whisk the remaining dry ingredients together. Add them to the wet ingredients and mix until just combined.

Roll the dough into 1-inch/2.5 cm balls. Start with a heaping tablespoon of dough, or use a 1-tablespoon cookie scoop. Arrange the dough balls no more than 12 to a pan, so that they have some room to spread. Using the back of a melon baller or a round measuring spoon that will make fairly round indentations in the cookies, press wells for the jam into the cookies. Spoon ½ teaspoon of jam into each hollow.

Bake the cookies for 12 to 14 minutes, or until they're golden brown. Cool briefly on the baking sheets and then transfer the cookies to wire racks to finish cooling.

These cookies will keep for up to 5 days in an airtight container. For longer storage, layer them in a freezer-safe container between layers of parchment and freeze.

Note: I tested these cookies with almond and sunflower seed butters and they both worked beautifully.

VEGAN JAMMY OATMEAL PECAN BAR COOKIES

MAKES 24 BARS

This is a cookie first introduced to me by my former intern, Olivia. She prefers to roll the dough into individual balls and make them into traditional thumbprint cookies. While I admit that they might look prettier that way, baking them up as a bar cookie is far less work and makes them into a viable recipe candidate for parties and potlucks. I particularly rely on this recipe when I'm asked to bring something to vegan or kosher gatherings, as it's entirely plant-based. You can even make them gluten-free by swapping certified GF oat flour in for the whole wheat.

RECOMMENDED PRESERVES:
Choose something that's got a bit of a tang to it. The cookie dough is so rich that it needs something bright and acidic to balance it. Marmalades and cranberry-centric jams are both really good options.

1½ cups/180 g pecans

1½ cups/150 g rolled oats

1½ cups/170 g whole wheat flour

1 teaspoon fine sea salt

¾ cup/140 g coconut oil

¾ cup/180 ml pure maple syrup

¾ cup/180 ml jam

Preheat the oven to 350°F/177°C.

Put the pecans and oats in the work bowl of a food processor and process until they have a grainy consistency. Add the whole wheat flour and salt and pulse to combine. Then, add the coconut oil and maple syrup and process until well combined.

Scrape the dough into a large bowl and push it into a ball with your hands. If the coconut oil didn't integrate all the way while in the food processor, knead it in now.

Take two thirds of the dough and press it into an even layer in the bottom of a 13 x 9-inch/33 x 23 cm baking pan.

Spoon the jam onto the dough and use an offset spatula to spread it out evenly. Crumble the remaining dough loosely on top of the jam, aiming for as even coverage as possible.

Although it won't darken dramatically, bake until the topping has browned a bit and is set, 45 to 50 minutes.

Remove the pan from the oven and let it cool. Cut into bars and serve. Covered with plastic or foil, these will keep for up to 5 days on the counter. For longer storage, wrap well and freeze.

BLUE CHEESE JAM SQUARES

MAKES 48 SMALL SQUARES

Looking for something to serve with drinks at your next party? These little sweet and savory squares should rocket to the top of your list. They're essentially a shortbread bar cookie. However, instead of making an all-butter dough, you swap in some pungent, crumbly blue cheese. The result is a slightly salty, sophisticated take on a traditional jam bar.

RECOMMENDED PRESERVES:
Opt for something sweet and strongly flavored. I like these with cherry, plum, or blackberry jam. Subtler flavors have a hard time holding their own against the cheese.

1 cup/120 g all-purpose flour, plus more for dusting

5 ounces/140 g cold, unsalted butter

3 ounces/85 g crumbled blue cheese (about ¾ cup)

½ teaspoon freshly ground black pepper

½ cup/120 ml jam

In the work bowl of a food processor, combine the flour, butter, blue cheese, and pepper. Process until the dough just starts to come together and begins to form a ball. Scrape the dough out of the food processor bowl and shape into a disk. Swaddle the dough in plastic wrap and refrigerate for at least an hour and up to 3 days. This dough can also be frozen for 3 to 4 months, if double wrapped in plastic.

When you're ready to bake, preheat the oven to 350°F/177°C. Line a 13 x 9-inch/33 x 23 cm baking pan with parchment paper, leaving the paper ends protruding to overhang the pan on 2 opposite sides.

Divide the dough into quarters. Set aside one of the quarter portions to use as the topping. On a lightly floured surface, roll out the remaining three quarters of the dough into a rough sheet about ¼ inch/6 mm thick and work it into the lined baking pan.

Spread the jam evenly on top of the dough. Crumble the reserved dough into bits (or grate it with a box grater) and distribute it over the top of the jam. Bake until the top is nicely browned, 40 to 45 minutes. Remove from the oven and let cool.

When the dough has cooled enough that moving it isn't going to break the base, at least 30 to 45 minutes, run a knife around the edges and then lift the bars out of the pan, using the overhanging parchment. Cut into 48 small squares with a large knife or a pizza cutter. These will keep for up to 5 days on the counter in an airtight container. For longer storage, freeze.

SHORTBREAD BARS

MAKES 24 COOKIES

I was born into a family that loves Christmas cookies that are studded with toasted nuts, bits of chocolate, dried fruit, and lots of jam. Various versions of the Rugelach (page 150) are our ideal. However, I married a man who prefers basic cookies and would rather go without than eat a cookie that contains raisins. In the beginning, I tried to convince him that our cookies were delicious. Eventually, I gave up trying to change his palate and started baking batches of shortbread instead.

RECOMMENDED PRESERVES:
My husband likes these unadulterated, but I prefer them eaten with a dollop of lemon curd or a sticky swipe of apricot jam.

1 cup/225 g unsalted butter, at room temperature

¾ cup/150 g granulated sugar

2 teaspoons vanilla extract

2 cups/240 g all-purpose flour

1 teaspoon fine sea salt

½ cup/120 ml jam or lemon curd

Preheat the oven to 325°F/163°C. Line a 13 x 9-inch/33 x 23 cm baking pan with parchment paper, leaving the paper ends protruding to overhang the pan on 2 opposite sides.

Place the butter, sugar, and vanilla the bowl of a stand mixer fitted with the paddle attachment and cream together until the mixture is pale yellow and fluffy, 2 to 3 minutes.

Add the flour and salt to the bowl and run the mixer on low speed until it is just incorporated.

Scrape the dough onto the prepared baking pan. Press the dough evenly into the pan and prick it repeatedly with the tines of a fork to prevent it from rising.

Bake for 40 to 45 minutes, or until the top is an even, golden brown.

Run a butter knife around the edges to loosen the cookie. Let it cool for 10 to 15 minutes so that it firms up a bit. Using the overhanging parchment paper, lift the cookie out onto a cutting board. Cut into even squares while the cookies are still warm enough to be pliable. If you let them cool completely, they will shatter messily rather than giving you clean, sharp lines. Serve topped with a teaspoon of jam or lemon curd.

Once the cookies are completely cool, store them in an airtight container. They will keep for at least 1 week on the counter. For longer storage, wrap them in plastic and freeze.

JAM-SWIRLED BROWNIES

ॐ

MAKES 16 SMALL BROWNIES

I have a battered aluminum baking pan in my kitchen that once belonged to my Great-Aunt Doris. She used this pan exclusively for her brownies and my mother and her cousins still associate the sight of it with the smell of chocolate. They were all mightily disappointed the first time I used it to transport grilled vegetables to a family gathering. This recipe isn't exactly the one Aunt Doris used to make, but with its ribbon of jam, it is equally crowd-pleasing.

RECOMMENDED PRESERVES:
Berry and grape preserves are my favorites here, but if you can imagine the preserve tasting good with chocolate, it should work.

½ cup/110 g unsalted butter, plus more for pan

2 ounces/60 g unsweetened chocolate

1 cup/170 g semisweet chocolate chips, divided

½ cup/100 g granulated sugar

2 large eggs

1 teaspoon vanilla extract

½ cup/60 g all-purpose flour

½ teaspoon fine sea salt

3 tablespoons jam

Preheat the oven to 350°F/177°C. Butter an 8-inch/20 cm square baking pan.

Using a double boiler or a stainless-steel mixing bowl positioned over a saucepan of simmering water, melt the butter, unsweetened chocolate, and ⅔ cup/110 g of the semisweet chocolate chips together. When they're melted, remove the bowl from the saucepan and let the melted chocolate cool down a bit.

Once the bowl is cool enough to touch, add the sugar and whisk to combine. Next, whisk in the first egg and then the second. Finally, add the vanilla.

In a small bowl, whisk the flour and salt together. Add to the wet ingredients and whisk to combine. Finally, stir in the reserved ⅓ cup/60 g of chocolate chips.

Scrape the brownie batter into the prepared pan and use an offset spatula to smooth out the top. Gently bang the pan a few times to work out any trapped air bubbles.

To distribute the jam into the brown batter, visualize a rectangular tic-tac-toe board on top of the pan, and place a teaspoon dollop of jam in the middle of each section. Using a butter knife, swirl the jam throughout batter.

Bake the brownies until the corners begin to pull away from the pan and the edges are slightly browned, 30 to 35 minutes.

Let them cool completely before slicing.

PUMPKIN BUTTER CHEESECAKE BARS

MAKES 24 BARS

When my mom was growing up, Saturday was frozen cheesecake night. After dinner, my grandma would take a frozen Sara Lee cheesecake out of the deep freeze and plunk it, still frozen, on the kitchen table. The five of them would then chip away at the cake with their forks as it defrosted. When I was young, I tried to convince my mother that we should carry on the frozen cheesecake tradition. Sadly, she denied my requests, but would occasionally make these bars as a treat.

RECOMMENDED PRESERVES:
Pumpkin butter makes these bars a dead ringer for pumpkin cheesecake, but they're also delightful when made with pear or peach butter.

24/370 g graham crackers

½ cup/110 g melted butter

½ cup/100 g granulated sugar

1 (8-ounce/228 g) package cream cheese, at room temperature

2 large eggs

1 (14-ounce/397 g) can sweetened condensed milk

1½ cups/420 ml pumpkin butter

1 teaspoon pumpkin pie spice

½ teaspoon fine sea salt

Preheat the oven to 350°F/177°C. Line a 13 x 9-inch/33 x 23 cm baking pan with parchment paper, leaving the paper ends to protrude and overhang the dish on 2 opposite sides.

Place the graham crackers into the work bowl of a food processor and pulse until pulverized into fine crumbs. Add the melted butter and sugar and process just until all the crumbs start to clump. Scrape the crumbs into the lined baking dish and press them into an even layer.

Using a stand mixer fitted with a paddle attachment, or a hand mixer, beat the cream cheese until it is fluffy. Add the eggs, sweetened condensed milk, pumpkin butter, pumpkin pie spice, and salt. If you're using a stand mixer, switch to the whisk attachment and beat until the cheesecake batter is entirely smooth. If you have white flecks in the batter, you'll have white flecks in the finished bars.

Pour the batter over the crust and use an offset spatula to smooth the top. Bake until the cheesecake is set, 55 to 60 minutes. It should still wobble gently, but shouldn't be at all liquid.

Remove from the oven, cool completely in the baking dish, and then move it to the refrigerator to chill. When you're ready to serve, run a knife around the edges of the baking dish to loosen and use the overhanging parchment to lift the bars out of the pan. Cut into 24 bars and serve. Any leftover bars should be stored in the refrigerator.

SWIRLED MERINGUE COOKIES

MAKES 24 COOKIES

In my father's family, no birthday dinner is complete without Pinch Pie, a dessert constructed from a sculpted meringue shell, ice cream, sweetened strawberries, whipped cream, and toasted flaked almonds. It's an incredibly sweet treat that I adored when I was young. While I still love the concept of Pinch Pie, I find that my tastes have changed enough in adulthood that I can't stomach more than a few bites. Instead of giving it up entirely, I've taken my favorite bits (the meringue and the fruit) and turned it into a cookie.

RECOMMENDED PRESERVES:
To my taste buds, this cookie demands strawberry or raspberry jam. However, for those without my strong flavor associations, just about any tasty, well-set jam will work here.

4 large egg whites, at room temperature

½ teaspoon cream of tartar

⅔ cup/130 g granulated sugar

½ teaspoon vanilla extract

½ cup/120 ml jam

Preheat the oven to 250°F/121°C. Line 2 rimmed baking sheets with parchment paper.

Pour the egg whites into the bowl of a stand mixer fitted with a whisk attachment. Make sure your mixer bowl and whisk attachment are squeaky clean. Even a trace of oil can prevent the egg whites from inflating properly. Add the cream of tartar and turn the machine to a medium-high speed. When the whites are looking frothy and have increased in volume a little, slowly stream in the sugar as the machine continues to run. Stop the mixer once to scrape down the bowl. Once the sugar is incorporated, add the vanilla.

Continue to whip the egg whites until they reach the stiff peak stage, 4 to 5 minutes. The meringue should look very glossy, feel heavy, and should stand up proudly from the whisk.

Remove the bowl from the machine. Using a silicone spatula, gently fold in the jam. Don't try to mix it in uniformly. Take care to leave some streaks of white.

Using 2 soup spoons, dollop the meringue about 1 inch/2.5 cm apart onto your lined baking sheets. You should be able to get 12 cookies onto each pan. Using your finger, swirl each cookie into a messy peak. You can also get this same effect with a piping bag, but I find that to be a lot of fuss for a simple treat.

Bake for 75 to 90 minutes, swapping the position of the pans at least once while baking. The cookies should brown around the edges and feel lighter than they did when they went into the oven. When you touch the surface of a finished cookie, it will feel smooth. If it still feels sticky or tacky, it's not done yet. If you've used really fresh egg whites that have a higher moisture content, it could take as long as 1½ hours for the cookies to finish baking. The cookies won't be as dry as commercially made meringues, but instead should have a bit of chew on the interior.

Remove the pans from the oven. The cookies will sink a little as they cool. Let the cookies cool completely. If they stick to the parchment slightly, as they might, use a spatula. They'll keep in an airtight container on your countertop for up to 5 days, though the texture will soften slightly over time.

QUICK STRUDEL

MAKES 2 LARGE STRUDELS, EACH SERVING 12 TO 14

My Great-Aunt Doris made finger food the way other women garden or take tennis lessons. She was always on the hunt for a new recipe, a unique serving platter, or a source for discount Pepperidge Farm thin-sliced white bread. When she wasn't working as a nurse or volunteering at her synagogue, you'd find her in the kitchen, cooking to fill her deep freeze. While many of her other creations have drifted into foggy memory, this strudel still regularly appears at family gatherings.

RECOMMENDED PRESERVES:
Apricot jam is traditional, but nectarine or plum is also good.

2 cups/240 g all-purpose flour, plus more for dusting

8 ounces/225 g unsalted butter, at room temperature

1 cup/240 ml sour cream

1 teaspoon fine sea salt

1 cup/240 ml jam

1½ cups/180 g chopped pecans or walnuts, toasted

1 cup/150 g golden raisins

1 large egg

In the work bowl of a food processor, combine the flour, butter, sour cream, and salt. Run the processor until the dough forms a ball. Spread a sheet of plastic wrap out on the countertop and scrape the dough onto the plastic. Wrap the dough tightly and refrigerate until firm, about 1 hour.

When you're ready to make the strudels, remove the dough from the fridge and preheat the oven to 350°F/177°C. Line a rimmed baking sheet with parchment paper.

Generously dust your work surface with flour. Divide the dough in half and place the first portion on the floured area. Roll the dough around the flour to coat, forming it into a chunky rectangle as you move it.

Using a well-floured rolling pin, gently work the dough into a 14- to 15-inch/36 to 38 cm square. Make sure that the dough isn't sticking to the board by using plenty of flour.

Divide the jam, nuts, and raisins in half. Whisk the egg with 1 tablespoon of water. Pour ½ cup/120 ml of the jam onto the prepared dough and spread it out to cover, leaving a 1-inch/2.5 cm border along the edge farthest from you. Distribute the nuts and raisins evenly across the jam-covered territory. Starting at the edge closest to you, begin to roll the dough toward the border. Wrap as tightly as you can without tearing the dough.

When you've reached the other side, paint the border with some of the egg wash and roll the strudel to close. Roll the strudel so that the seam is on the bottom. Pinch the ends to seal and carefully move the strudel to the prepared baking sheet.

Repeat the process with the second batch of dough, jam, nuts, and raisins.

When both strudels are on the baking sheet, paint the tops generously with the egg wash. Bake until the tops are deeply golden and the smell of toasted butter becomes impossibly delicious, 40 to 46 minutes.

Remove the pan from the oven and let the strudels cool on the baking sheet for 10 to 15 minutes. Carefully slide the parchment from each baking sheet to a wire rack to finish cooling.

When fully cool, slice the strudels into 1-inch/2.5 cm pieces. They will keep on the counter for 3 to 4 days. For longer storage, leave the strudel unsliced, triple wrap them in plastic, and stash them in the freezer for up to 6 months.

LINZER BAR COOKIES

MAKES 24 SQUARES

Traditional Linzer cookies are carefully rolled and cut sandwich cookies, filled with generous dollops of raspberry jam. They are delicate, beautiful, and somewhat of a pain to get right. However, I love a lightly sweet and buttery almond cookie with jam. So, some years back I took a batch of Linzer dough, pressed most of it into a quarter sheet pan, gave it a slick of jam, and topped it with rounds of the remaining dough, and baked it. The result was a bar cookie that was easy to slice between the rounds into squares and was awfully good. I like to use mini cookie cutters for the dough on top. This ends up giving them a reverse Linzer look, with the jam showing around the edges rather than through a hole in the top round.

RECOMMENDED PRESERVES: *Raspberry is classic, but I've made these with peach, apricot, or orange marmalade. It's hard to go wrong here.*

½ cup/60 g raw blanched almond slivers

1½ cups/180 g all-purpose flour, plus more for sprinkling

½ teaspoon baking powder

Lightly toast the almonds in a dry skillet over medium heat for 5 to 7 minutes. You don't want to get a lot of color on them; you just want to bloom their natural oils, bring out some fragrance, and warm them up a little to make them more receptive to grinding.

Pour the warm almonds into the work bowl of a food processor and pulse 7 or 8 times, or until they resemble rough meal. Add the flour, baking powder, and salt and pulse until just combined.

In the bowl of a stand mixer fitted with the paddle attachment, beat the butter and sugar together until

½ teaspoon fine sea salt

6 ounces/170 g unsalted butter,
  at room temperature

⅔ cup/135 g granulated sugar

1 large egg

1 teaspoon vanilla extract

½ cup/120 ml jam

light and fluffy, 3 to 4 minutes. Add the egg and vanilla and beat just until combined.

Add the dry mixture to the wet ingredients in the stand mixer and run on low just until the ingredients are incorporated.

Spread a length of plastic wrap on your countertop and carefully scrape the cookie dough into the plastic. Using the edges of the plastic, form the dough into a rough disk. Refrigerate for at least 1 hour before using and up to 24 hours.

When you're ready to make your cookies, preheat the oven to 325°F/163°C. Line a 13 x 9-inch/33 x 23 cm baking sheet with parchment paper so that the paper edges protrude to overhang on 2 opposite sides. Divide the dough into 2 portions: one that is one third of the total; and the other, two thirds.

Dust your work surface with some flour and roll out the larger portion of dough into a rectangle that's about the same size at the bottom of the pan and about ⅛ inch/3 mm thick. Transfer the dough into the pan, pressing it into place and patching any tears that occur.

Spoon the jam onto the cookie dough and use an offset spatula to even and smooth.

Roll out the remaining dough into a similar thickness. Use cookie cutters to cut the dough into shapes and tile them across the jam, leaving some jam peeking through.

Bake for 22 to 25 minutes, or until the tops of the cookies are light brown and the jam is glossy.

Remove the pan from the oven and let the cookie slab cool to room temperature in the pan. Using the overhanging parchment paper, lift the slab out of the pan and place it on a cutting board. With a sharp knife, cut into individual cookies.

These cookies will keep in an airtight container for a week on the counter and up to 6 months if frozen.

HAMANTASCHEN

MAKES 12 TO 16 COOKIES

When I was in high school, my mom came home with a 2-pound bag of pitted prunes so she could make her favorite prune Hamantaschen for Purim. She thought she had put the bag far enough back from the edge of the counter, but our dog managed to get ahold of it, and in less than five minutes, polished off every last prune. The dog learned the hard way that she should stay away from prunes and I learned that it's better to make Hamantaschen with jam.

RECOMMENDED PRESERVES:
These triangle cookies like jams and fruit butters with relatively stiff consistency. If you have any overset preserves, use them here.

4 ounces/110 g unsalted butter, at room temperature

4 ounces/110 g cream cheese, at room temperature

¼ cup/50 g granulated sugar

½ teaspoon vanilla extract

1¼ cups/150 g all-purpose flour, plus more for dusting

¼ teaspoon fine sea salt

½ cup/120 ml jam

1 large egg, beaten with 1 tablespoon water

In the bowl of a stand mixer fitted with the paddle attachment, combine the butter, cream cheese, and sugar and beat on medium-high speed until pale and fluffy. Add the vanilla and beat again until combined.

In a medium mixing bowl, combine the flour and salt and whisk together. Add the dry ingredients to the wet and mix on low speed just until the flour is incorporated.

Scrape the dough onto a length of plastic wrap, swaddle tightly, and refrigerate for at least 1 hour and up to 24 hours.

When you're ready to make the cookies, divide the dough into 2 equal-size portions. Dust your work surface with flour and roll out the dough until it about ¼ inch/6 mm thick. Cut the dough into circles, using a 3-inch/7.5 cm round cutter. Dollop a teaspoon of jam in the center of each circle and brush the uncovered edges of the cookie with the egg wash (the egg wash functions as a glue as well as a coating). Shape each circle into a triangle by pinching the edges and pulling the sides of the dough up over the filling, so that only a shirt button–size area of the jam remains visible. They should look like little tricorn hats. Really pinch the edges tightly and roll the seams down slightly to seal in the jam.

Put the filled and shaped cookies on a plate and place them in the freezer to chill for an hour. Repeat with the remaining dough. Make sure to refrigerate the egg wash while the cookies chill, as you will need it again and you don't want it to spoil in the interim.

Preheat the oven to 350°F/177°C. Place the chilled cookies on a baking sheet lined with parchment paper or silicone baking mat. Paint the cookies with the egg wash to give them an appealing sheen.

Bake the cookies for 20 to 25 minutes, or until the dough is nicely browned and the jam looks glossy and sticky. The sides of the cookie will inevitably have opened up a little, but if you pinched and sealed the sides tightly enough, most should retain their triangular shape. Don't fret if one or two cookies open completely during baking. It happens to the best of us.

Transfer the cookies to a wire rack to cool. They'll keep for up to a week in an airtight container.

Note: A big tip of the hat to my friend Deena Prichep, who taught me to freeze these cookies a few at a time on a plate, rather than trying to squeeze a baking sheet into my already overstuffed freezer.

RUGELACH

MAKES 32 TO 36 COOKIES

This is the cookie of my mother's people. Her Auntie Tunkel always had a tin of them in her valise-size handbag when she visited, most often filled with jam, raisins, and nuts. I often make them at my sister's house when we gather for the holidays and they are always the first to disappear from the jar. My favorite thing about these cookies is that they're made with an unsweetened dough, so all the sweetness comes from the jam. If you don't have much of a sweet tooth, use fruit butter or a very lightly sweetened jam to match your taste.

RECOMMENDED PRESERVES:
I like these with apricot or tart cherry, but any jam you've got on hand should work.

2 cups/240 ml all-purpose flour, plus more for dusting

½ teaspoon fine sea salt

8 ounces/225 g cold unsalted butter, diced

8 ounces/225 g cold cream cheese, diced

¾ cup/180 ml jam

¾ cup/90 g finely chopped pecans or walnuts, toasted

1 large egg, beaten with 1 tablespoon water

Granulated sugar and ground cinnamon, for dusting

Place the flour and salt in the work bowl of a food processor. Pulse 2 to 3 times to combine. Add the butter and cream cheese and process until the dough forms a rough ball.

Scrape out the dough and shape into a disk. Swaddle the dough ball in plastic wrap and refrigerate for at least 1 hour and up to 3 days. The dough can also be frozen for 3 to 4 months, if double wrapped in plastic.

When you're ready to make the rugelach, preheat the oven to 375°F/190°C. Line a baking sheet with parchment paper or silicone baking mat.

Divide the chilled dough into 3 portions. Dust your countertop with flour and roll out one portion of dough into a rectangle about ¼ inch/6 mm thick. Spread a third of the jam onto the rolled dough, leaving a ½-inch/1.25 cm border along one of the long sides. Distribute a third of the toasted nuts on top of the jam.

Paint the border of dough with the egg wash. Roll the dough toward it, keeping the roll as tight as possible. When you get to the edge that's been painted with the egg wash, push it down to seal.

Position the roll so that the seam is facing down. Paint the top of the roll with the egg wash and sprinkle it with sugar and cinnamon. Repeat with remaining dough and filling.

Using a knife with a serrated edge, cut the roll into sections of about ¾ inch/4 cm in width. Place them, seam-side down, spaced about an inch/2.5 cm apart, on the lined baking sheet.

Bake for 20 to 25 minutes, or until they are browned and flaky. Some of the filling will inevitably leak out.

Let the cookies cool for at least 15 minutes before you attempt to move them, as they are quite fragile when hot.

The cookies will keep in an airtight container for up to 1 week. For longer storage, arrange them in a freezer-safe container with parchment dividing the layers.

Once you've made a basic batch, consider trying some variations. Here are a few ideas you can use as a starting place.

APRICOT JAM ᴀɴᴅ WALNUT RUGELACH

Use ¾ cup/180 ml of apricot jam and ¾ cup/90 g of finely chopped and toasted pecans or walnuts.

TOMATO JAM ᴀɴᴅ GOAT CHEESE RUGELACH

Use ¾ cup/180 ml of tomato jam and 3 ounces/85 g of cold, crumbled goat cheese.

GRAPE JAM ᴀɴᴅ PEANUT RUGELACH

Use ¾ cup/180 ml of grape jam and ¾ cup/90 g of finely chopped and toasted peanuts.

CAKES, PUDDINGS, AND COBBLERS

I didn't realize that jams were often used for filling cakes until I was in high school. A group of us had shown up at my friend Kate's house on a Saturday afternoon with a box of cake mix, intending to both go swimming in Kate's family pool and bake a cake. We started making the cake, but got distracted with swimming and splashing, and left the baking project undone.

Later in the afternoon, I wandered back to the kitchen, and found Kate's mom, Lenore, assembling our cake for us. She put a dab of frosting on the plate to hold the first layer in place and then spooned raspberry jam onto the cake. Watching her spread the jam, stack the next layer, and finish the cake with frosting felt instructive, meditative, and soothing, particularly in contrast to the sounds of happy shouts and splashing coming from the backyard.

When I ate my slice, I noticed how the jam served as a sharp, tart complement to the sweet layers of cake and frosting. I've been tucking jam and other preserves into cakes ever since.

That said, not all of the following collection of cakes, puddings, and cobblers employ jam as Lenore did that day. Some of the cakes do use it as a filling. Others use applesauce, marmalade, fruit butter, or whole preserved fruit. There are even a couple of recipes in this section that don't include a lick of preserves in the actual dessert, but instead are made complete when served with a generous dollop of jam.

VICTORIA SANDWICH

MAKES ONE 8-INCH/20 CM LAYER CAKE

Until I started watching *The Great British Baking Show*, I had no idea how many classic English desserts and pastries included generous portions of jam. There are trifles, jam roly-polies, summer puddings, bakewell tarts, and even the evocatively named Queen of Puddings (layers of custard, cake, and jam, topped with meringue), but my personal favorite will always be the Victoria sandwich. Made from two rounds of gorgeously light pound cake and sandwiched together with jam and whipped cream, it is easy to make and a delight to eat. My only major change to the traditional approach is that I like to add a little tang to the whipped cream in the form of crème fraîche or sour cream. It helps cut through and balance the sweetness of the jam.

RECOMMENDED PRESERVES:
Raspberry jam is traditional, but I've also used strawberry or blackberry to delicious effect.

¾ cup/170 g unsalted butter, at room temperature, plus more for pans

¾ cup/150 g granulated sugar

3 large eggs, at room temperature

2 tablespoons whole milk

½ teaspoon vanilla extract

1⅓ cups/160 g all-purpose flour

1 tablespoon baking powder

½ teaspoon fine sea salt

1 cup/240 ml heavy whipping cream

3 tablespoons confectioners' sugar, divided

¼ cup/60 ml crème fraîche or sour cream

½ cup/120 ml berry jam

Preheat the oven to 325°F/163°C. Generously butter two 8-inch/20 cm round cake pans and line the bottoms with a circle of parchment paper.

In the bowl of a stand mixer fitted with the paddle attachment, cream the butter and sugar together for 3 to 4 minutes, stopping to scrape down the sides occasionally. Once it looks light and fluffy, beat in the eggs, one at a time. Add the milk and vanilla and mix until combined.

In a medium mixing bowl, whisk together the flour, baking powder, and salt. Add the dry ingredients to the wet ingredients and mix until just incorporated, then stop the mixer. It's imperative that this cake has a light texture and too much mixing can make it tough.

Divide the cake batter evenly between the 2 prepared pans. Use an offset spatula to smooth out the batter.

Bake for 35 to 40 minutes, or until the cakes are lightly browned on top and a cake tester comes out clean when inserted into the center of a cake (a few crumbs are fine, wet batter is not).

Remove from the oven and let the cakes cool in the pans for a few minutes, then turn them out onto a wire rack, positioned so that the tops are facing up.

You want to have at least one cake with a gorgeous top and rack impressions don't look pretty.

While the cakes are cooling, pour the cream into the cleaned bowl of the stand mixer fitted with the wire whisk. Add 2 tablespoons of the confectioners' sugar and whip on medium speed. When you've reached the stiff peak stage, turn off the mixer and remove the bowl. Fold in the crème fraîche with a silicone spatula.

To assemble the cake, place the less per-fect of the 2 layers on a plate or cake stand, bottom-side up. Spread the jam across the cake as evenly as you can. Dollop half the whipped cream mixture over the jam and use an offset spatula to make it even and smooth. You can also use a pastry bag, but they're bothersome to clean, so I employ them only when absolutely necessary. Place the second cake round gently on top of the whipped cream, making sure that this cake round is top-up. Top the cake with the remaining whipped cream. Slice and serve!

YOGURT UPSIDE-DOWN CAKE

MAKES ONE 10-INCH/25 CM CAKE

We've all heard tell of those cakes that can be stirred together in the moments it takes for an unexpected guest to park their car and walk to the house. I'm not sure that this one is quite that quick (I guess it all depends on how long the path is to your front door), but it's blessedly speedy nonetheless. I make it using a single bowl, a whisk, a cast-iron skillet, and whatever jam is currently open in the fridge.

RECOMMENDED PRESERVES:
I find that this cake is best made with chunkier jams or compotes, but truly, anything can be used. I particularly like it with thick-cut marmalade. Arrange the bits of orange rind in spiral pattern if you're feeling artistic.

1 cup/240 ml plain whole-milk Greek yogurt

½ cup/120 ml neutral oil

3 large eggs

1 teaspoon vanilla extract

1¼ cups/250 g granulated sugar

1½ cups/180 g all-purpose flour

2½ teaspoons baking powder

1 teaspoon fine sea salt

1 cup/240 ml jam

Preheat the oven to 350°F/177°C. Oil a 10-inch/25 cm cast-iron skillet or a similarly sized deep, round cake pan. Cut a round of parchment paper and place it in the bottom of the skillet.

In a large bowl, whisk together the yogurt and oil until well combined. Add the eggs and vanilla and whisk. Add the sugar and whisk. Add the flour, baking powder, and salt and whisk to combine.

Pour the jam onto the parchment round in the prepared skillet, spread it to coat, and carefully spoon the cake batter over the jam, trying not to displace too much of the jam. Smooth with an offset spatula.

Bake for 35 to 40 minutes, rotating the cake at least once during baking so that it bakes evenly. The cake is done when the top is nicely browned and a cake tester inserted into the center comes out mostly clean (a few moist crumbs are okay).

Remove the cake from the oven and let it cool for 5 minutes or so in the skillet. Run a knife around the edges of the cake to loosen.

Put a plate over the skillet and, using hot pads to protect your hands, invert the cake onto the plate. It's important to do this relatively soon after the cake comes out of the oven, so that it doesn't stick. Carefully peel the sheet of parchment away from the cake with a spatula in hand, so that you can push bits of the jam back into place, as necessary.

Serve warm.

MARMALADE POUND CAKE

MAKES 2 LOAVES

When Scott and I were planning our wedding, one of the things I was really clear on was that I wanted to bake our dessert. We did not have the budget to buy an exceptional cake and I was not willing to serve lackluster cake to our friends and family. And so, in the days before our big day, I baked a dozen cakes. Half were loaves of this pound cake and the remaining six were Flourless Chocolate Cake (page 162). A decade later, my in-laws still mention our delicious wedding cakes whenever I see them. It was well worth the work!

RECOMMENDED PRESERVES:
Marmalade. Any kind. If it's really thick-cut, consider dicing the big hunks of peel before stirring into the batter.

1½ cups/340 g unsalted butter, at room temperature, plus more for pans

3 cups/360 g all-purpose flour, plus more for pans

2½ cups/495 g granulated sugar

2 tablespoons grated orange zest

8 large eggs, at room temperature

⅓ cup/80 ml marmalade

1 tablespoon vanilla extract

1½ teaspoons baking powder

1 teaspoon fine sea salt

GLAZE

¾ cup/85 g confectioners' sugar

⅔ cup/160 ml marmalade

½ cup/120 ml water

Preheat your oven to 325°F/163°C. Butter and lightly flour two 8 x 4-inch/20 x 10 cm loaf pans.

Using a stand mixer fitted with the paddle attachment, cream the butter, sugar, and orange zest together for 3 to 4 minutes, or until fluffy.

Break the eggs into a spouted measuring cup. With the mixer running on a moderate speed, add the eggs, one at a time. When the eggs are incorporated, add the marmalade and vanilla and beat them in.

In a medium mixing bowl, whisk together the flour, baking powder, and salt. Add the flour mixture to the batter and mix just until combined, stopping to scrape down the sides of the bowl with a silicone spatula, as needed. Remove the bowl from the mixer and stir a few times to ensure that the flour from the edges of the bowl and any runnier batter from the bottom are all blended in.

Divide the batter evenly between the 2 prepared pans and smooth the tops.

Bake the cakes for 35 minutes. When the time is up, rotate the pans 180° so that the cakes bake evenly. Continue to bake until a cake tester comes out mostly clean from the center of a cake (a few crumbs are okay), another 30 to 35 minutes.

While the cakes bake, prepare the glaze: In a small pan, combine the confectioners' sugar, marmalade, and water. Place over medium heat and warm until everything melts together.

Remove the pans from the oven and place them on a wire rack set over a baking sheet. Let them cool for 10 to 15 minutes and then remove the cakes from the pans. Set them, top-side up, on the rack and spoon the glaze over the warm cakes. Use a brush to glaze the sides of the cakes. Keep spooning and brushing until all the glaze has been distributed over the cakes.

Let them cool completely before serving.

Note: I find that these cakes improve with age. If you can manage it, bake them at least a day or two before serving. They also freeze beautifully, if left unglazed.

FLOURLESS CHOCOLATE CAKE

SERVES 16 TO 20 IN SMALL, RICH SLICES

I have made this cake more times than I can count. I served it at my wedding with raspberry sauce and a gallon of freshly whipped cream. We made half a dozen when my sister got married. I've taken it to birthday parties, potlucks, Passover Seders, and funeral meals. It is easy to make, improves with age, travels well, and can be offered to people who don't eat gluten. While it can be served just as it is, I like to warm up a half-pint of jam and pour it over the top of the cake just before slicing. It soaks in just a bit and makes for glorious leftovers. This cake is also excellent when topped with a billowing cloud of the Raspberry Fool (page 170).

RECOMMENDED PRESERVES: *This cake goes best with raspberry or cherry jam. Strawberry does in a pinch, but doesn't always hold up to the intensity of the chocolate.*

1 cup/225 g unsalted butter, cubed, plus more for pan

8 ounces/225 g semisweet chocolate, broken into bits

1½ cups/300 g granulated sugar

6 large eggs

1 cup/85 g unsweetened cocoa powder

¼ cup/60 ml hazelnut liqueur (e.g., Frangelico) or strong brewed coffee

1 cup/240 ml berry jam

Preheat the oven to 350°F/177°C. Generously butter a 9-inch/23 cm springform pan and line the bottom with a circle of parchment paper.

Create a double boiler by setting a large glass or stainless-steel bowl over a saucepan with 2 to 3 inches/5 to 7 cm of water in the bottom. Make sure that the bottom of the bowl isn't in the water. Place the double boiler over medium-high heat. Place the chocolate and butter in the bowl and let melt. Stir to help them combine.

Once the chocolate and butter have melted, remove the bowl from its perch on the saucepan and place it on a folded kitchen towel. Using a hand mixer, whisk in the sugar.

Break the eggs into a spouted measuring cup and add them, one at a time, as the mixer runs.

Sift the cocoa powder into the batter and, starting on the mixer's lowest setting and slowly work upward, beat to combine. Finally, beat in the liqueur.

Scrape the batter into the prepared pan. Gently knock the pan on your counter a few times to coax out some of the air bubbles.

Bake until a cake tester comes out mostly clean (a few crumbs are fine, wet batter is not), 45 to 50 minutes. If the top cracks, don't worry about it.

Remove the cake from oven and let cool in the pan for at least 20 minutes before carefully removing it from the pan. If you don't plan on serving it immediately, wrap it in 2 or 3 layers of plastic wrap and store in the refrigerator or freezer until you're ready to serve. Allow cake to come to room temperature prior to serving. Just before slicing, pour the berry jam over the top.

Note: This cake freezes really well, both whole and in slices. I have small, individually wrapped slices in my freezer even as I type.

FRUIT BUTTER DOLLOP CAKE

SERVES 9

This cake is based on Marian Burros's famous Plum Torte. It's a recipe that has run in the *New York Times* on numerous occasions and is a summertime classic. I've adapted it slightly by using preserves rather than fresh plums, making it accessible for year-round cooking. I encourage you to think creatively about the various preserves with which you stud the cake batter. My suggestion of fruit butter is a delicious one, but you could also use berries canned in syrup or some of the whole fruit you stashed in the freezer with every intention of making jam at a later date.

RECOMMENDED PRESERVES:
To start, I highly suggest trying this cake with plum or peach butter. From there, the world is yours to explore.

½ cup/110 g unsalted butter, at room temperature, plus more for baking dish

1 cup/120 g all-purpose flour

2 teaspoons ground cinnamon

1 teaspoon baking powder

½ teaspoon freshly grated nutmeg

½ teaspoon fine sea salt

1 cup/200 g granulated sugar

2 large eggs

¼ cup/60 ml fruit butter

Preheat the oven to 350°F/177°C and lightly butter an 8-inch/20 cm square Pyrex baking dish.

Whisk together the flour, cinnamon, baking powder, nutmeg, and salt in a medium bowl and set aside.

Using either a stand mixer fitted with the paddle attachment or a hand mixer, cream together the sugar and butter for 2 to 3 minutes, or until light and fluffy. Add the eggs and beat to combine. Add the dry ingredients to the wet and mix until they are just combined.

Scrape the batter into the prepared baking dish. Working in a 4 x 4 grid pattern and using 2 teaspoons (one to scoop and hold the butter, and the other to push it off the spoon), place 16 small rounds of fruit butter on top of the batter. Resist the urge to swirl in the fruit butter and instead leave the dollops intact, to reduce the risk of burning.

Bake until the corners of the cake pull away from the baking dish slightly and a toothpick inserted into the center of the cake (avoiding the puddles of jam) comes out clean, 50 to 55 minutes.

Remove the cake from the oven and let it cool to room temperature. Serve straight from the baking dish.

Note: The fruit butter may sink into the batter during baking. That's okay. As you cut the cake, you'll uncover tasty pools of fruit, which are delicious.

CHOCOLATE APPLESAUCE CAKE

SERVES 9 TO 12

This cake is a humble, homely thing. When it is finished baking, the top is cracked, craggy, and lacking in any kind of shine. However, the first taste always makes up for any visual deficits. It is moist, rich, and just gets better with age. It's the cake I bake when I'm craving something sweet and don't want to indulge too much.

RECOMMENDED PRESERVES:
If you don't have apple-sauce, try this cake with any unsweetened fruit sauce. For a sweeter cake with a fudgier texture, replace the apple-sauce with puréed strawberry preserves.

6 tablespoons/85 g unsalted butter, at room temperature, plus more for baking dish

¾ cup/150 g granulated sugar

2 large eggs

1 cup/245 g unsweetened applesauce

1 teaspoon vanilla extract

1 cup/120 g all-purpose flour

½ cup/55 g unsweetened cocoa powder

1½ teaspoons baking powder

½ teaspoon baking soda

½ teaspoon fine sea salt

Preheat the oven to 350°F/177°C. Butter an 8-inch/20 cm square Pyrex baking dish and set aside.

Using a hand mixer or a stand mixer fitted with a paddle attachment, beat the butter and sugar together for 2 to 3 minutes, or until light and fluffy. Add the eggs, applesauce, and vanilla and beat to combine.

In another bowl, sift together the flour, cocoa powder, baking powder, baking soda, and salt. Add the dry ingredients to the wet and stir on low to combine. Scrape the sides of the bowl down and beat until smooth.

Pour the batter into the prepared baking dish and smooth the top to level. Bake until the top domes, the edges pull away from the baking dish, and a cake tester inserted into the center comes out clean, 35 to 40 minutes.

Remove the baking dish from the oven and place it on a wire rack to cool. Serve warm or at room temperature. Any leftover cake will keep in an airtight container on the counter for up to 5 days. For longer storage, refrigerate or freeze.

CHOCOLATE SAUERKRAUT CAKE

MAKES 1 LARGE BUNDT CAKE

I know that the idea of a chocolate cake shot through with sauerkraut sounds off-putting at first glance, but I promise, this cake isn't a gimmick. It's actually a fairly traditional recipe that is said to have originated in the days when schools and institutions got big cans of government surplus sauerkraut and needed to find ways to use it creatively. However it came to be, the result is a tasty, tender cake in which the kraut serves as a textural component that mimics the feel of shredded coconut. The finished cake tastes hearty and grounded, with only the smallest hint that you stirred fermented cabbage into the batter.

RECOMMENDED PRESERVES:
Basic sauerkraut, well drained.

Oil, for pan

2¼ cups/270 g all-purpose flour

¾ cup/83 g unsweetened cocoa powder

1 teaspoon baking powder

1 teaspoon baking soda

½ teaspoon fine sea salt

4 ounces/110 g unsalted butter, at room temperature

1½ cups/300 g granulated sugar

3 large eggs, at room temperature

1 teaspoon vanilla extract

1 cup/180 g drained Basic Sauerkraut (page 227)

1 cup/240 ml water

Preheat the oven to 350°F/177°C degrees. Generously oil a Bundt pan.

In a medium bowl, whisk together the flour, cocoa powder, baking powder, baking soda, and salt.

Using a hand mixer or a stand mixer fitted with the paddle attachment, cream together the butter and sugar until light and fluffy, 3 to 4 minutes. Add the eggs and vanilla and mix until well combined.

Rinse the sauerkraut under running water and drain. Place it in a blender with the fresh water and run the machine until the sauerkraut is well chopped.

Add the sauerkraut slurry to the bowl of wet ingredients and mix to combine.

Add the flour mixture to the wet ingredients in stages, mixing on low speed, just until combined.

Pour the batter into the prepared Bundt pan and bake until a cake tester inserted in the center comes out mostly clean (a few dry crumbs are okay), 40 to 45 minutes.

Remove from the oven and let the cake cool completely in the pan on a wire rack, then invert the cake onto a plate.

APPLE BUNDT CAKE

MAKES 1 LARGE BUNDT CAKE

I bake this cake in early fall, when apples are fresh and I want to celebrate the arrival of slightly cooler days. It's also one of those cakes that can do double duty. It's just as good eaten as part of a brunch spread as it is served at the end of a meal, with a spoonful of barely sweetened whipped cream. The end result is a really satisfying, versatile cake.

RECOMMENDED PRESERVES:
I make this cake with thick, homemade apple butter. If you feel like pears rather than apples, use a combination of thick pear butter and fresh pears in their place.

- 5 ounces/140 g unsalted butter, at room temperature, plus more for pan
- 1 cup/120 g all-purpose flour, plus more for pan
- 1 cup/110 g whole wheat flour
- 2 teaspoons baking powder
- ½ teaspoon baking soda
- ½ teaspoon fine sea salt
- ½ teaspoon ground cinnamon
- ¼ teaspoon freshly grated nutmeg
- 1¼ cups/250 g granulated sugar
- 2 large eggs
- 1 cup/240 ml apple butter
- 2 medium-size apples, peeled, cored, and grated (about 2 cups/480 ml)
- 1 tablespoon grated fresh ginger
- 1 cup/120 g toasted and chopped walnuts
- ½ cup/80 g golden raisins

Preheat the oven to 350°F/177°C. Generously butter and flour a 12-cup/2.8 L Bundt pan.

Whisk together the flours, baking powder, baking soda, salt, cinnamon, and nutmeg in a bowl.

Using a hand mixer or a stand mixer fitted with the paddle attachment, cream the butter and sugar together for 3 to 4 minutes, or until light and quite fluffy.

Break the eggs into a spouted measuring cup. With the mixer running on a moderate speed, add the eggs, one at a time. When the eggs are incorporated, add the apple butter, grated apples, and ginger. Mix to incorporate.

Add the dry ingredients in a few additions, mixing just until they are combined. Finally, add the nuts and raisins and mix until they are dispersed.

Scrape the batter into the prepared Bundt pan and level the top with a silicone spatula.

Bake until a tester inserted into the center of the cake comes out clean, 55 to 60 minutes.

Remove from the oven and set the pan on a wire rack to cool. When the cake is fully cooled, place the rack over the top of the cake pan and flip to remove from the pan. Well wrapped, the cake will keep in the refrigerator for up to 1 week.

Note: If you don't have a Bundt pan, this cake can also be made in a pair of loaf pans.

LAYERED BREAD PUDDING

SERVES 8 TO 10

For the longest time, I was opposed to bread pudding. I thought it was a throwaway dessert, something you make only when you couldn't manage anything better. Then I tasted really good bread pudding and I changed my tune. Now it's a dessert I crave and I'm always searching for reasons to make a batch.

RECOMMENDED PRESERVES:
Strong flavors are best here. I like raspberry, blackberry, or cherry. You could also transform this into a savory dish by omitting the sugar and vanilla and layering the bread with chutney and grated cheese.

6 tablespoons/85 g unsalted butter, melted, divided

12 slices store-bought white sandwich bread, cut into triangles (about 1 pound/ 450 g bread)

¾ cup/180 ml jam

4 large eggs

2 cups/480 ml whole milk, plus more if needed

⅓ cup/65 g granulated sugar

½ teaspoon vanilla extract

Preheat the oven to 375°F/190°C. Brush a 13 x 9-inch/33 x 23 cm baking dish with 1½ tablespoons of the melted butter.

Arrange one third of the bread across the bottom of the prepared baking dish. Using an offset spatula, spread half of the jam evenly over the bread. Drizzle with 1½ tablespoons of the melted butter. Layer in another third of the bread and spread the remaining jam. Drizzle with 1½ tablespoons of the melted butter.

Arrange the remaining third of the bread on top and drizzle with the remaining 1½ tablespoons of melted butter. Place the baking dish on a rimmed baking sheet. In a medium bowl, whisk the eggs, milk, sugar, and vanilla together and slowly pour over the layered bread. If you're working with fresh bread, it will seem as though the egg mixture won't fit in the baking dish at first, but the bread will absorb it all when given the chance. If your bread is quite stale and soaks up the custard so hungrily that the top slices of bread aren't well saturated, drizzle them with an additional ½ cup/120 ml of milk. You can also use a large spoon or spatula to gentle compress the bread to help the top slices get their fair share of the liquid.

Leaving the baking dish on the baking sheet, transfer both to the oven. Bake until the top of the pudding puffs up and is a deep, golden brown, 30 to 35 minutes. It should look like a gloriously burnished grilled cheese sandwich and the custard should be nicely set.

If the top is golden but there's still a lot of liquid in the baking dish, cover the top with a piece of aluminum foil and continue to bake.

Remove the baking dish from the oven and let the pudding cool just a little before serving. It is best eaten within half an hour of leaving the oven, but it does reheat deliciously.

Note: For a dish that is more like a French toast casserole and less like bread pudding, use 6 eggs and 1½ cups/360 ml of milk. It's also good with a dusting of cinnamon and nutmeg. My mom often sprinkles raisins and nuts between each layer when she makes it to serve at breakfast.

CREAMY RICE PUDDING

SERVES 6 TO 8

I have always been an equal-opportunity rice pudding lover. Be it store-bought or made with brown rice left over from dinner (often my mother's approach), I will happily slurp up a bowlful. However, no rice pudding pleases me more than this one. It's built on the bones of versions shared by Elizabeth David and Laurie Colwin and is the perfect creamy foil for tangy jams, butters, and curds. When I'm feeling extra indulgent, I finish the pudding by stirring in some heavy cream. However, if you're reaching for something lighter, the pudding is still very good without it.

RECOMMENDED PRESERVES:
Top this pudding with lemon curd, lightly sweetened plum preserves, or my favorite, cranberry sauce leftover from Thanksgiving.

¾ cup/150 g uncooked arborio rice

4 cups/960 ml whole or 2% milk

⅓ cup/67 g granulated sugar

1 vanilla bean, split and scraped

¼ teaspoon fine sea salt

½ cup/120 ml heavy whipping cream (optional)

Preheat the oven to 250°F/121°C.

Place the rice, milk, sugar, vanilla bean seeds and pod, and salt in an oven-safe casserole dish. Stir to combine.

Place the dish, uncovered, in the oven and bake, stirring every 30 minutes, for 2 hours.

Remove the pudding from the oven, pluck out the vanilla bean pod, and stir in the cream, if using. The pudding will seem quite soupy at this stage, but as it cools, it will begin to thicken. If you can wait an hour, it will end up being gorgeously creamy and thick.

Serve hot, warm, or cool, topped with a generous dollop of tart preserves.

RASPBERRY FOOL

SERVES 6 TO 8

When I was in high school, the Rimsky-Korsakoffee House was one of my favorite places to go with friends. Located on the ground floor of an old Victorian mansion in southeast Portland, it was funky, charming, and welcoming to packs of teenagers, provided we didn't get too raucous. My favorite thing on the menu was the Chocolate Raspberry Fool. Served in a sundae glass, it was a cloud of raspberry-studded whipped cream, interrupted with layers of chocolate drizzle. This version is a straight-out homage and is particularly delicious when served with the Flourless Chocolate Cake (page 162).

RECOMMENDED PRESERVES:
In my opinion, raspberry jam is the only way to go, but you could also use blackberry, gooseberry, or even cranberry jam.

1½ cups/420 ml heavy whipping cream

3 tablespoons confectioners' sugar

2 cups/280 g fresh raspberries, plus more for garnish

2 tablespoons granulated sugar

¼ cup/60 ml raspberry jam

2 ounces/55 g dark chocolate, for grating on top

Pour the cream into the bowl of a stand mixer fitted with a whisk attachment or a large bowl, and sift in the confectioners' sugar. Turn on the mixer or use a hand mixer to whip until the cream reaches stiff peaks. This is firmer than you typically take whipped cream, so be brave, but cautious. (See note.)

While the mixer runs, combine the raspberries with the sugar and mash them together with a fork. Once the berries look juicy, stir in the jam.

When the cream is stiff, remove the bowl from the mixer and fold in the berry mixture. I like to leave it streaky, rather than try to get a uniform mix.

To serve family style, spoon the finished fool into a pretty glass bowl and use a rasp-style zester to grate the chocolate over the top. It's also fun to spoon the fool into individual ramekins or dessert cups and sprinkle those with the grated chocolate. It can be made and kept in the fridge up to 24 hours in advance of serving.

Note: Make sure to be attentive to your cream as it whips so that you don't overwhip it. However, if you get distracted and your cream breaks into butter and buttermilk, don't get upset. Pour the butter curds into a fine-mesh strainer, rinse with cold water, and squeeze out the buttermilk. Serve the sweetened butter at your next brunch gathering and tell everyone you did it on purpose!

FRUIT COBBLER

SERVES 8 TO 10

I grew up in a household that preferred nubbly, fruit-centric desserts. I tried to re-create those crisps for this book, but found that preserved fruit didn't partner well with crumbly toppings. So, I went looking for other techniques that would transform the home canned fruit into easy and satisfying desserts. Surprisingly, I found it in the movie *Steel Magnolias*. Remember the scene in which Truvy (played by Dolly Parton) describes her cuppa, cuppa, cuppa cake? This is essentially that, made with added butter for richness, a little less sugar, and a whole lot more fruit.

RECOMMENDED PRESERVES:
Any preserved fruit will work here. You can also use your frozen fruit for this recipe, if you prefer.

4 ounces/110 g unsalted butter

1 cup/120 g all-purpose flour

¾ cup/150 g granulated sugar

1½ teaspoons baking powder

½ teaspoon fine sea salt

1 cup/240 ml whole milk

1 teaspoon vanilla extract

3 cups/720 ml drained canned fruit

Preheat the oven to 350°F/177°C. Put the butter in a 13 x 9-inch/33 x 23 cm Pyrex baking dish and pop it into the oven to melt.

Combine the flour, sugar, baking powder, and salt in a blender. Add the milk and vanilla and purée on low speed until the batter is smooth.

Once the butter has melted, carefully remove the baking dish from the oven. Arrange the fruit in a single layer over the butter.

Pour the batter over top of the fruit and butter, using a spatula to even it out, if necessary.

Bake for 35 to 40 minutes, or until the edges turn brown and pull away from the sides of the baking dish. The center should be just set.

Serve hot, warm, or at room temperature. It's particularly good with some plain yogurt or a dollop of soft whipped cream.

SPICED PEACH COBBLER
Add 2 teaspoons of ground cinnamon and ½ teaspoon of grated nutmeg to the batter. Arrange 3 cups/750 g of drained canned peaches in the bottom of baking dish.

PEAR AND CRANBERRY COBBLER
Arrange 2 cups/500 g drained of canned pear slices and 1 cup/110 g of fresh or drained pickled cranberries in the bottom of the baking dish.

BLUEBERRY AND WALNUT COBBLER
Arrange 3 cups/750 g of drained canned blueberries and ½ cup/60 g of toasted and chopped walnuts in the bottom of the baking dish.

PIES AND TARTS

One of the best things about being known among my friends and acquaintances as a lover of home preserves is that people report back when they discover particularly interesting jam applications. Several years back, my friend and fellow food writer Deena Prichep sent me an excited chain of texts. She had just interviewed a baker who always added jam to the fruit she tucked into her hand pies. This baker felt that the pectin helped firm up the filling in a way that allowed her to use less thickeners. This revelation sent me down a jam-filled-pie rabbit hole and I spent months filling various piecrusts with jams, compotes, and even pickled fruit. The results of that obsession are recorded in this chapter, along with a savory tart, a fruit-filled tart, and a pie that's half jam, half berries. May your explorations be equally delicious.

FAVORITE PIECRUST

MAKES ENOUGH FOR A STANDARD DOUBLE-CRUST PIE
OR A 13 x 9-INCH/33 X 23 CM SLAB PIE

This is the piecrust I use most often. I've been making it since early 2005, when I got my hands on a copy of *The Martha Stewart Cookbook*. I figured if a crust was good enough for Martha, it was good enough for me. I like that it's relatively sturdy yet always manages to bake up beautifully. I use this crust for most of my pies, hand pies, and all my savory tarts (it does contain a pinch of sugar, but it's not so much that it makes the crust sweet).

2½ cups/300 g all-purpose flour

1 teaspoon fine sea salt

1 teaspoon granulated sugar

8 ounces/225 g cold, unsalted butter

3 to 4 tablespoons ice-cold water, or as needed

Place the flour, salt, and sugar in the work bowl of a food processor and pulse to combine. Cut the butter into small pieces and add it to the flour mixture. Pulse 5 or 6 times to help break up the butter. Then, with the motor running, stream in 3 tablespoons of the water. If the dough doesn't seem to be coming together, add up to the final tablespoon. Stop processing the moment you see the dough beginning to form blueberry-size clumps.

Spread a length of plastic wrap on your countertop and carefully scrape the messy dough into the plastic. Using the edges of the plastic, form the dough into a rough disk. Refrigerate for at least 1 hour before using. The dough will keep in the fridge, tightly wrapped, for several days. The dough can also be frozen for up to 6 months.

SWEET TART CRUST

MAKES ENOUGH FOR TWO 9-INCH/23 CM TARTS

For tarts that I plan on filling with lemon curd, jam whipped with cream cheese, or the Raspberry Fool (page 170) topped with more fresh raspberries, this is the crust I bake. It is crisp yet tender and always does justice to the filling. Just know that this one is a little fussy to roll out. Often I skip the rolling pin entirely, break off small pieces, and just press it into the pan with damp fingers rather than risk the frustration.

2½ cups/300 g all-purpose flour

3 tablespoons granulated sugar

1 teaspoon fine sea salt

8 ounces/225 g cold, unsalted butter

2 large egg yolks, beaten

3 to 4 tablespoons ice-cold water

Place the flour, sugar, and salt in the work bowl of a food processor and pulse to combine. Cut the butter into small pieces and add it to the flour mixture. Pulse 5 or 6 times to help break up the butter. Then, with the motor running, add the egg yolks and then stream in 3 tablespoons of the water. If the dough doesn't seem to be coming together, add up to the final tablespoon. Stop processing when you see the dough beginning to form blueberry-size clumps.

Spread a length of plastic wrap on your countertop and carefully pour the dough into the plastic. Using the edges of the plastic, form the dough into a rough disc. Refrigerate for at least 1 hour before using. The dough will keep in the fridge, tightly wrapped, for several days. The dough can also be frozen for up to 6 months.

JAM SLAB PIE

MAKES ONE 13 X 9-INCH/33 X 23 CM PAN

A slab pie is one that is made on a rimmed baking sheet rather than in a traditional pie plate. Because the pan has less height, the ratio of filling to crust is different from that of a conventional pie. For those who prize generous portions of flaky crust, it's a welcome change. Additionally, much like sheet cakes, slab pies also have the ability to easily delight a hungry crowd of eaters.

RECOMMENDED PRESERVES: *I've made this slab with peach, sour cherry, or plum jam or conserve and they've all been wonderful. If your jam is very chunky, you can skip the compote. I recommend it here simply to give the filling some texture.*

1 recipe Favorite Piecrust (page 176)

All-purpose flour, for dusting

3 cups/720 ml jam

1 cup/240 ml fruit compote or drained canned fruit (roughly chop if pieces are large)

2 tablespoons cornstarch

1 large egg, beaten with 1 tablespoon water

Preheat the oven to 400°F/204°C. Position a 13 x 9-inch/33 x 23 cm rimmed baking sheet (also known as a quarter sheet pan) next to your work area.

Divide the pie dough into 2 equal-size portions. Dust your work surface with flour and roll out one half of the dough into a large enough rectangle to line the baking sheet, with a little bit of overhang. Loosely roll the dough around your rolling pin and then unroll it over the baking sheet. Ease the crust into the corners of the pan and patch any tears that appear.

In a medium mixing bowl, stir the jam, compote, and cornstarch together. Scrape it into the prepared piecrust and spread it to the inner edges.

Roll out the remaining portion of the pie dough into a large enough rectangle to cover the pan. Roll the crust loosely around your pin and unfurl it over the pie filling. Tuck the edges in and crimp the crust. Cut a series of vents in the top of the crust. Paint the top of the pie with the egg wash.

Bake for 30 minutes. When that time is up, lower the heat to 350°F/177°C and bake until the filling bubbles up through the vents, the edges of the pie begin to pull away from the corners of the pan, and the top of the crust is a gorgeous brown, an additional 15 to 20 minutes.

Remove the pie from the oven and let it cool to room temperature before you attempt to slice it.

HAND PIES

Hand pies are essentially homemade Pop-Tarts. They can be as simple or fancy as you choose and are a great way to use up leftover pie dough and the ends of a few jars of jam. Despite the fact that they're actually easier to make than a full-size pie, they manage to feel like an extra-special treat. Next time you need to cheer up a co-worker or your spouse, make them a hand pie. I promise it will lift their mood and make them feel appreciated.

RECOMMENDED PRESERVES:
Any tasty jam you've got open.

1 recipe Favorite Piecrust
(page 176)
All-purpose flour, for dusting
1¼ cups/300 ml jam
1 large egg, beaten with
1 tablespoon water
1 to 2 tablespoons turbinado
sugar, or as needed

Preheat the oven to 400°F/204°C. Line a pair of rimmed baking sheets with parchment paper or silicone baking mats.

Divide the pie dough into 2 equal-size portions. Dust your work surface with flour and roll out the dough into a 12 x 8-inch/30 x 20 cm rectangle. Cut the dough into eight 4 x 3-inch/10 x 8 cm rectangles.

Portion 2 tablespoons of jam into the center of 4 of the pastry rectangles. Paint the edges of the rectangle with the egg wash and then place another piece of pastry on top. Crimp the edges with the tines of a fork to seal. Prick the top 2 or 3 times with the fork to give the hot air a place to escape. Repeat with the remaining rectangles.

Place the completed hand pies on the lined baking sheet and paint the tops with the egg wash. Sprinkle with the sugar.

Place the first baking sheet in the oven while you prep the second half of the dough. Reroll leftover dough to make additional pies.

Bake until the pies are golden on top and have puffed slightly, 35 to 40 minutes. Remove them from the oven and let them cool on the pan for a few minutes and then carefully transfer them to a wire rack to finish cooling.

Finished pies are best eaten within the first 24 hours, but will keep for 3 to 4 days in an airtight container.

FRESH AND JAMMED STRAWBERRY PIE

MAKES ONE 9-INCH/23 CM PIE

Strawberry pie is one of the great pleasures of early summer. However, I often get a hankering for a strawberry pie in February, when small, ruby-hued strawberries exist only in my memory. When that happens, I pull out a jar of strawberry jam, settle for strawberries shipped up from Florida, and treat myself to a pie worthy of summer.

RECOMMENDED PRESERVES:
Strawberry jam. If yours is very runny, increase the amount of cornstarch by a tablespoon.

1 recipe Favorite Piecrust (page 176)

All-purpose flour, for dusting

3 pounds/1.4 kg fresh strawberries, hulled and diced

2 cups/480 ml strawberry jam

3 tablespoons cornstarch

1 large egg, beaten with 1 tablespoon water

Preheat the oven to 400°F/204°C. Position a 9-inch/22 cm pie plate next to your work area.

Divide the pie dough into 2 equal-size portions. Dust your work surface with flour and roll out the dough into a round large enough to line your pie plate. Loosely roll the dough around your rolling pin and then unroll it over the dish. Carefully ease the crust into the dish and patch any tears that appear.

In a medium mixing bowl, stir the strawberries, jam, and cornstarch together. Spoon it into the prepared piecrust.

Roll out the remaining pie dough into another large round. Roll the crust loosely around your pin and unfurl it over the filling. Trim the edges and crimp the crust. Cut a series of vents in the top of the crust. Paint the top of the pie with the egg wash.

Place the pie in the oven and bake for 30 minutes. When that time is up, lower the heat to 350°F/177°C and bake until the filling bubbles up through the vents, the edges of the pie begins to pull away from the corners of the pan, and the top of the crust is a gorgeous brown, an additional 15 to 20 minutes.

Remove the pie from the oven and let it cool to room temperature before you attempt to slice it.

Note: You don't have to use a single sheet of piecrust to cover this one. You could weave a lattice or cut shapes out with cookie cutters and layer them on top. It's up to you.

FANCY JAM TART

SERVES 10 TO 12

The bones of this tart comes from a blog post that David Lebovitz wrote more than ten years ago and I've been making versions of it ever since. The thing that makes it so special is the cornmeal in the crust—it makes the texture pleasingly sandy. I like to make this tart in a removable-bottom tart pan, but if you don't have one, you could also use a square baking dish and cut the tart into small squares, as you would a bar cookie.

RECOMMENDED PRESERVES: *Any jam with a solid set serves well here. I particularly like how damson plum or sour cherry go with the almond extract in the dough.*

4 ounces/110 g unsalted butter, at room temperature

½ cup/100 g granulated sugar

1 large egg

1 large egg yolk

½ teaspoon almond extract

1½ cups/180 g all-purpose flour

½ cup/70 g finely ground cornmeal

½ teaspoon fine sea salt

2 teaspoons baking powder

2 cups/480 ml jam

In the bowl of a stand mixer fitted with the paddle attachment, combine the butter and sugar and beat on medium-high speed until pale and fluffy. Add the egg, egg yolk, and almond extract and beat again until combined.

Place the flour, cornmeal, salt, and baking powder in a medium mixing bowl and whisk until combined. Add the dry ingredients to the wet ingredients in 3 portions, beating to combine between additions.

Gather the dough into a ball and divide into 2 portions, one of them two thirds of the total; and the other, one third. Shape the 2 dough balls into disks, wrap in plastic, and refrigerate for at least 1 hour and up to 24 hours.

When you're ready to construct the tart, remove the dough from the fridge and preheat the oven to 375°F/190°C. Take the larger portion of dough and press it directly into the bottom and halfway up the sides of a 9-inch/22 cm removable-bottom tart pan. (It's a pretty crumbly dough. Attempting to roll it out can lead to heartache.)

Spoon the jam into the prepared dough and spread it evenly with an offset spatula. Using your fingers, break off small bits of the remaining dough and scatter them over the jam, much like you would with a crumble or streusel topping.

Place the tart pan on a rimmed baking sheet to catch any potential bubbling jam. Bake for 25 to 30 minutes, or until the crust is deeply brown, the topping has spread nicely, and the jam is bubbling.

Remove from the oven and allow to cool on a wire rack for 15 to 20 minutes, then remove the tart ring. If you wait until the tart is completely cool, any jam that bubbled onto the ring will stick and make it hard to remove. Let the tart cool completely before cutting and serving.

GOAT CHEESE AND SAVORY JAM TART

MAKES ONE 10 X 2-INCH/25 X 5 CM TART

Savory jams are still something of a mystery to most home cooks. They're not as easy to categorize and pin down as the classic all-sweet preserves. However, I firmly believe that having a few jars of tomato or onion jam in the pantry can be a boon to home cooks. You can pair them with cheese and crackers for an easy party appetizer. They give moisture to sandwiches when you're out of mayo. And when added to a tart like this one, they help make a dish you can be proud to serve to your fanciest friends.

RECOMMENDED PRESERVES:
I make this tart with Tomato Jam (page 219), some chutneys, or nearly any sweet and pungent onion condiment that winds up in my pantry. The basic rule of thumb is that you want something not too sweet and that pairs well with cheese.

All-purpose flour, for dusting

½ recipe Favorite Piecrust (page 176)

8 ounces/225 g creamy goat cheese

1 cup/240 ml heavy whipping cream

Preheat the oven to 350°F/177°C.

Dust your work surface with flour and roll out the crust into a round roughly 14 inches/35 cm in diameter. Loosely roll the crust around your pin and unfurl it over a 10 x 2-inch/25 x 5 cm removable-bottom tart pan. Tuck the crust into the corners of the pan and trim away overhanging dough. Crumple up a sheet of parchment paper and then spread it out over the molded dough. Fill the parchment with pie weights or dried beans that you save for this purpose. Bake the crust for 20 to 25 minutes, or until it is set, but not significantly browned. While it bakes, make the filling.

In a medium saucepan, combine the goat cheese and cream. Heat over low heat, stirring to work the cheese into the cream, until the mixture is fairly uniform. Remove the pan from the stove and let it cool for a few minutes. Whisk 3 tablespoons of the cheese

2 large egg yolks, beaten

2 garlic cloves, minced or
pressed

1 tablespoon chopped fresh
rosemary

1 tablespoon chopped fresh
thyme

1 teaspoon fine sea salt

¼ teaspoon freshly ground
black pepper

3 tablespoons finely diced
shallot

1 cup/240 ml savory jam, such
as tomato or onion

mixture into the beaten egg yolks, 1 tablespoon at a time, to temper the eggs. Stir the tempered eggs into the cheese mixture. Add the garlic, rosemary, thyme, salt, and pepper.

Remove the pie weights from the tart shell, place it on a rimmed baking sheet, and pour in the filling. Sprinkle the shallots across the top of the filling, trying to keep them on the surface, rather than letting them sink. Increase the oven temperature to 375°F/190°C and bake the filled tart for 25 to 30 minutes, or until it is just set.

Remove the tart from the oven and spread the savory jam on top, using an offset spatula to create a smooth, even surface. Return the tart to the oven and bake for an additional 8 to 10 minutes, just to warm the jam and help it meld with the rest of the tart.

Remove from the oven and let the tart cool for at least 30 minutes before slicing. Serve warm or at room temperature.

LEMON CURD & BLUEBERRY TART

MAKES ONE 9-INCH/23 CM TART

I have always loved a good grocery store fruit tart. Traditionally made from layers of pastry cream, carefully arranged berries, and a perfectly clear glaze, they are one of my favorite things to bring to a party when I'm pressed for time and can't manage something homemade. However, if I've got time to create something at home, I go a little less traditional. The bright, smooth lemon curd is many times more interesting than pastry cream, and the blueberries look pretty and rustic (with no fussy arranging required).

RECOMMENDED PRESERVES: *I like this tart when it's made with lemon curd and blueberries, but it works equally well with other kinds of curds and different varieties of berries. Just know that if you use berries that you have to chop, which will release lots of juice, the tart won't hold as long before serving as one made with intact berries.*

All-purpose flour, for dusting

½ recipe Sweet Tart Crust (page 177), chilled and ready to roll

2 cups/480 ml lemon curd

12 ounces/340 g fresh blueberries

2 to 3 tablespoons lemon or apple jelly, or as needed, for glazing

Preheat the oven to 350°F/177°C.

Dust your work surface with flour and roll out the crust into a round roughly 12 inches/30 cm in diameter. Loosely roll the crust around your pin and unfurl it over a 9-inch/23 cm removable-bottom tart pan. Tuck the crust into the flutes of the pan and trim away any excess crust. Prick the bottom of the dough with a fork to help prevent air bubbles from forming. Crumple up a sheet of parchment paper and then spread it out over the molded dough. Fill the parchment with pie weights or dried beans that you save for this purpose. Bake the crust until it is light brown and isn't at all damp looking, 20 to 25 minutes.

Remove the crust from the oven and let it cool to room temperature.

To fill, pour the lemon curd into the shell and spread it evenly, using an offset spatula.

Rinse the blueberries and check them carefully for stems and dried-up blossoms. Dry them thoroughly and pour them into a mixing bowl. Warm the jelly just until it is loose enough to be pourable and drizzle it over the berries. Toss until they are well coated and gently tumble them evenly over the lemon curd.

Serve chilled.

DRINKS

Drinks and cocktails are one of the places where a homemade pantry can really shine. All manner of beverages can be made better and more interesting with a dollop of jam, marmalade, or shrub. During the summer months, I adopt the habit of swirling homemade syrups or runny jellies into tall glasses of sparkling water. In winter, I love to stir homemade marmalade into a mug of freshly boiled water or tea sweetened with a little apple ginger syrup.

Because I don't personally drink much alcohol, I needed a little help when it came to developing some of these drinks, and my friend Emily Teel came to my rescue. She's a food writer and recipe developer who loves a good cocktail and she was instrumental in the creation of the following libations. We brainstormed together, pulled a bunch of jars from my pantry, and got to mixing and shaking. The first four recipes in this chapter are the result of this collaboration and they are far better creations than I'd have concocted on my own.

MEYER LEMON MARMALADE MARTINI

MAKES 1 MARTINI

The bittersweet nature of marmalade shines in this twist on a classic martini. This is a strong cocktail, so if alcohol goes to your head as quickly as it does mine, opt for the variation that has you serve it with a generous splash of club soda.

RECOMMENDED PRESERVES:
Floral Meyer lemon marmalade is lovely here, but you can make this with the marmalade of your choice.

2 ounces/60 ml gin or vodka

½ ounce/15 ml orange liqueur (Combier, Cointreau, or Grand Marnier)

½ ounce/15 ml freshly squeezed lemon juice

1 tablespoon Meyer lemon marmalade

Club soda (optional)

Lemon wheel or twist, for garnish

Fill a shaker with ice and add the gin, orange liqueur, lemon juice, and marmalade. Shake vigorously until the exterior of the shaker is frosty, 15 to 20 seconds. Strain the drink through a fine-mesh strainer, working the pulp with the back of a spoon to force as much of the liquid through as possible. Serve it up in a coupe or martini glass, or over fresh ice in a pint-size/500 ml jar topped with club soda, if using. Garnish with a lemon wheel or twist.

JAM BRAMBLE

MAKES 1 DRINK

A bramble is a classic gin cocktail typically made with blackberry liqueur and simple syrup. This version trades out both for blackberry jam, which gives the drink a vivid color and plenty of fruity sweetness. Three tablespoons might seem like a lot of jam for one drink, but a good deal of the fruit pulp is left behind when the drink is strained.

RECOMMENDED PRESERVES:
Blackberry jam is best here, but I could also see this made with black raspberry.

2 ounces/60 ml London Dry Gin (Beefeater or Tanqueray is best)

3 tablespoons/30 ml blackberry jam

2 tablespoons/30 ml freshly squeezed lemon juice

Fill a shaker with ice and add the gin, jam, and lemon juice. Shake vigorously until any whole berries in the jam are pulverized and the exterior of the shaker is frosty, about 20 seconds. Strain the drink through a fine-mesh strainer, working the pulp with the back of a spoon to force as much of the liquid through as possible. Serve it up in a coupe or martini glass, or over fresh ice in a pint-size/500 ml jar.

JAM DAIQUIRI

MAKES 1 DAIQUIRI

If you thought that daiquiris were a thing to be reserved for beach vacations only, think again. The sweetness in this one comes entirely from jam, blended with frozen fruit, white rum, lime juice, and ice. These proportions yield a generously sized, boozy cocktail. For a less powerful drink, or a nonalcoholic version, feel free to decrease the rum or omit it entirely, substituting water instead.

RECOMMENDED PRESERVES:
Strawberry is classic, but any other frozen fruit and jam combination could also work beautifully here. Try it with blueberries and blueberry jam, peaches and peach jam, or frozen pineapple with apricot jam.

Place all the ingredients in a blender and purée until totally combined and velvety. This would be the drink to garnish with a paper umbrella, if you've got one.

1 heaping cup/150 g frozen strawberries

¼ cup/60 ml strawberry jam

2 tablespoons freshly squeezed lime juice

⅓ cup/75 ml white rum

1 cup/140 g ice

BLUEBERRY BASIL LEMONADE HIGHBALL

MAKES 6 SERVINGS

This is simply a boozy lemonade that features a cheap party trick. As you build it in the glass, it develops a beautiful gradient effect for presentation. Serve with straws so your guests can swirl in the blueberry jam. A little sour on its own, this boozy lemonade gets balance from the jam. The crowd will love it.

RECOMMENDED PRESERVES: *Blueberry and lemon is a classic combination that's always perfect (for further proof, see the Lemon Curd and Blueberry Tart, page 186). You can also use strawberry, blackberry, or raspberry here, and this would be an excellent use for a fruit syrup, or a jelly that didn't quite set.*

1 cup/240 ml limoncello

½ cup/120 ml vodka

½ cup/120 ml fresh lemon juice

2 cups/480 ml cold or sparkling water

⅓ cup/80 ml blueberry jam

6 sprigs basil, mint, tarragon, or another fresh herb of your choosing

In a pitcher, stir together the limoncello, vodka, lemon juice, and water to create the lemonade. Divide the blueberry jam among 6 tall, highball-style glasses. Top the jam with ice to fill each glass. Gently pour the lemonade over the ice to fill each glass. Add a sprig of basil and a straw to each glass and serve.

Note: Feel free to mix the lemonade portion of this cocktail ahead of time. Store in the refrigerator until ready to serve.

MARMALADE HOT TODDY

MAKES 1 DRINK

This soothing drink is something I reach for whenever I'm not feeling well. Most of the time, I make it without the traditional bourbon so that it can be an all-day drink.

RECOMMENDED PRESERVES:
Lemon marmalade works best here, although lime is also nice.

2 tablespoons lemon marmalade

1 teaspoon freshly squeezed lemon juice

1 ounce/30 ml bourbon (optional)

1½ cups/355 ml just-boiled water

Combine the lemon marmalade, lemon juice, and bourbon, if using, in a large mug. Add the hot water and stir to combine.

Note: I sometimes also grate a little fresh ginger into my mug for added flavor. This is particularly good when you're battling a sore throat.

CHAMPAGNE SHRUB COCKTAIL

MAKES 6 COCKTAILS

Neither my husband nor I drink much alcohol, but we both love a glass of Champagne. I've taken to spiking glasses of champagne, prosecco, or domestic sparkling wine with a little homemade shrub to add flavor and interest to our favorite celebratory beverage. It's essentially a twist on the classic Kir Royale.

RECOMMENDED PRESERVES:
Fruit-forward shrubs are the thing to use here.

6 tablespoons shrub

1 (750 ml) bottle midrange Champagne, prosecco, or sparkling wine

Garnish to complement the shrub (e.g., whole or sliced fruit, or herb sprigs)

Line up 6 champagne flutes. Portion 1 tablespoon of shrub into the bottom of each glass. Fill each glass with about 4 ounces/120 ml of wine. Garnish as appropriate (see note). Serve.

Note: As far as the garnish goes, if you're using a blueberry shrub, float a few fresh blueberries in the glass to finish. If your shrub features citrus, garnish the glass with a twist of peel or a small wedge of fruit. It makes for a pretty finish and elevates the drink.

PANTRY SANGRIA

SERVES 6 TO 8

For most of my twenties, sangria was my drink. Every time my friends and I would gather for a party or cookout, I would make up a batch in a half-gallon jar to bring along. I liked it because it felt festive no matter the time of year and was a way to make even the most middling bottles of wine taste good. In this version, I've removed the traditional addition of sugar and replaced it with a little jam or marmalade to bring sweetness and a bit of flavor. I think it works beautifully!

RECOMMENDED PRESERVES:
I like marmalade or Concord grape jam, but you can be creative here. If you have some lemon syrup or an already-boozy jam, consider those as an option.

1 orange, sliced into thin half-moons

1 lemon, sliced into thin half-moons

½ cup/80 ml brandy

1 (750 ml) bottle red wine

¼ cup/60 ml marmalade or Concord grape jam

1 pound/450 g frozen grapes

Club soda, to serve

At least 8 hours before you plan on serving the sangria, combine the orange and lemon slices and the brandy in a jar to infuse. Refrigerate.

To build the sangria, combine the red wine and the marmalade in a container that can hold at least 2 quarts/1.9 L. Stir until the preserve melts into the wine. Add the soaked fruit and liquid to the wine and stir. Add the frozen grapes. Serve, and cut with club soda.

Note: During the winter, I sometimes leave out the frozen grapes and club soda, dilute the fruit/wine/brandy combination with a little water, warm it on the stove, and call it mulled wine. Somehow, it still works!

HERBAL FRUIT SPARKLER

MAKES 1 QUART/1 L

When it comes to hot summer days, my drink of choice is a quart-size jar, filled with a combination of ice, jam, muddled fresh herbs, and lots of sparkling water. It's the thing I make midafternoon to get me through the workday or on lazy weekend evenings when I'm sitting around with family. Often, I make a big batch in a pitcher when I'm having a potluck or dinner party. As time goes on, more and more of my friends are giving up booze, and it's a really good way to make them feel loved and cared for. I like to add fresh herbs to these sparkling drinks because they add a lot of flavor and do a good job of tempering the sweetness of the jam. You can always leave them out if you don't want bits of green floating in your drink, or if they just don't speak to you.

¼ cup/60 ml jam, jelly, or syrup

1 tablespoon soft, fresh herbs

1 cup/140 g ice

3 cups/720 ml sparkling water

In the bottom of a quart-size/1 L jar, combine the jam and herbs. Lightly stir the jam and herbs together. You want to bruise and soften the leaves, without tearing them into bits. Put the ice on top of the mixture and add the sparkling water. Stir to distribute, then serve.

APRICOT BASIL SPARKLER

¼ cup/60 ml apricot jam

6 to 7 fresh basil leaves

1 cup/140 g ice

3 cups/720 ml sparkling water

CHERRY MINT SPARKLER

¼ cup/60 ml cherry jam

10 to 12 fresh mint leaves

1 cup/140 g ice

3 cups/720 ml sparkling water

PINEAPPLE CILANTRO SPARKLER

¼ cup/60 ml pineapple jelly

2 to 3 sprigs cilantro

1 cup/140 g ice

3 cups/720 ml sparkling water

FROZEN TREATS

More than one of my childhood milestones had to do with food. My first sentence was "More mayonnaise, please" and the very first word I ever learned to spell was "ice cream." I was 18 months old and my parents had taken to spelling things so that I wouldn't catch on. Sadly for them, it didn't take long for me to find the key to their game and very soon, I could spell i-c-e c-r-e-a-m right along with them.

Although I'm a lifelong lover of frozen treats, I didn't start making ice creams and frozen yogurts until fairly recently. A big part of the reason is that as a food writer with a fairly small kitchen, I rarely had space in my freezer to get the ice-cream maker bowl in there for a good, solid chill. The other reason was that I didn't feel it was worth the investment of time and energy. However, the paradigm shifted when I invested in an ice-cream maker with a compressor and I realized that making sorbets, frozen yogurts, and ice creams with jams, jellies, and canned fruit was a giant shortcut. Normally, if you were making these frozen treats, you'd need to cook and cool any fruit before you could start freezing your treats. When you start with fruit that's already cooked and canned, you save so much time and deliver so much flavor.

PRESERVED PEACH SORBET

MAKES 4 CUPS/960 ML SORBET

This idea comes directly from my friend Audra Wolfe. As we both work from home, we have a weekly coffee shop date where we meet up to check in about our various projects before settling down to work for a couple hours. One summer day, she arrived, bursting with the news that a quart-size jar of peaches could be puréed with a little sugar and poured directly into an ice-cream maker for an excellent treat. I adopted the idea, tweaked it slightly, and am sharing it with you here.

RECOMMENDED PRESERVES:
I make this with the peaches I can in fruit juice or light syrup. If your fruit is canned in heavy syrup, consider backing off on the additional sugar. It also works with apricots, plums, nectarines, or pears.

3 cups/720 ml drained canned peaches (from 1 canned quart/liter), canning liquid reserved

2 tablespoons freshly squeezed lemon juice

¾ cup/150 g granulated sugar

Place the peaches into a blender and purée with the lemon juice. Measure out ½ cup/120 ml of the reserved peach canning liquid. If there's not enough, add water to make up the volume. Pour that liquid into a small saucepan and add the sugar. Heat over medium heat just until the sugar has melted.

Add the warm syrup to the peach purée in the blender and purée to combine. Pour the peach mixture into a container and refrigerate until cold, about 45°F/7°C. Freeze according to the manufacturer's directions for your ice-cream maker. When the sorbet is sufficiently frozen, transfer it to an airtight container, cover tightly, and freeze. It will keep for at least 1 week in the freezer.

ORANGE MARMALADE ICE CREAM

MAKES 5 CUPS/1.2 L ICE CREAM

One fall, Scott and I went to Ireland. It was a much-needed vacation after an intense year of caring for a sick relative and we reveled in our role as tourists. We wandered historic sites and stately homes, shopped for wool sweaters, and ate a diet heavy in fish, potatoes, brown bread, and ice cream. It was in an ice-cream shop in Killarney that I discovered the magic of marmalade ice cream. It was sweet, creamy, sharp, and bitter all at once. This recipe is the result of my many attempts to capture that flavor. I wouldn't say it's exactly right (Irish dairy is in a class all its own), but it's close enough and is definitely worth making.

RECOMMENDED PRESERVES:
Use a thick-cut orange marmalade the first time you make this and experiment from there.

2 cups/480 ml heavy whipping cream

1 cup/240 ml whole milk

½ cup/100 g granulated sugar

6 large egg yolks, beaten

1 teaspoon vanilla extract

⅛ teaspoon fine sea salt

½ cup/120 ml thick-cut marmalade, chilled in the refrigerator

In a medium saucepan, combine the cream, milk, and sugar and warm over medium heat, stirring regularly, until the sugar dissolves.

Remove the pan from the heat and let it cool for a few minutes. Add the warm cream mixture to the beaten eggs, 1 tablespoon at a time, until there's no risk of the warm mixture's scrambling the eggs. Then, add the remaining cream mixture. Return the mixture to the saucepan and cook over medium heat, whisking constantly, until it begins to thicken, 5 to 8 minutes. Add the vanilla and salt.

Pour the custard through a fine-mesh sieve set over a bowl to catch any curdled bits of egg. Refrigerate until cold, about 45°F/7°C. Freeze as instructed by your ice-cream maker.

When the ice-cream base is mostly frozen, fold in the cold marmalade. Transfer the ice cream to an airtight container, cover tightly, and freeze.

JAMMY FROZEN YOGURT

MAKES 5 CUPS/1.2 L FROZEN YOGURT

A few years back, there was a frozen yogurt boom in my neighborhood. Within a matter of months, four self-serve yogurt shops opened within a three-block radius of my apartment and if one closed, another would pop up in its place. Sadly, its popularity has waned (two of the yogurt shops were recently replaced by high-end pour-over coffee joints), but I'm okay with it because I can make my own frozen yogurt. A tub of runny, unsweetened yogurt, some sugar, and some jam, and I am set to start churning.

RECOMMENDED PRESERVES:
I like strawberry, raspberry, or cherry best.

3 cups/720 ml unsweetened whole-milk yogurt (not Greek-style yogurt)

1 cup/200 g granulated sugar

½ cup/120 ml jam

¼ teaspoon fine sea salt

Pour the yogurt, sugar, jam, and salt into a blender and purée. Pour the mixture into a container and refrigerate until cold, about 45°F/7°C. Freeze according to the manufacturer's instructions for your ice-cream maker. When the yogurt is sufficiently frozen, transfer it to an airtight container, cover tightly, and freeze. It will keep for at least 1 week in the freezer.

Note: The sugar in this recipe doesn't just sweeten the yogurt, it also helps maintain a scoopable consistency. You can reduce the sugar if you want, but know that the yogurt might harden and develop ice crystals while in the freezer.

RUNNY JELLY GRANITA

MAKES 3 CUPS/720 ML GRANITA

We all have a jar or two of jelly that never quite reached its potential. Whether it's just a bit soft or well and truly sloshy, when jelly fails the question is always, "What should I do with this?" You can always treat it as you would syrup and stir it into sparkling water or use it up at cocktail hour, but I'd like to offer another option—granita. This icy frozen treat is typically made with fresh fruit, sugar, and water, but I've found that delicious batches can be made using frozen fruit, runny jelly, and a little water. Best of all, this is one frozen treat that doesn't require an ice-cream maker or special mold. You freeze it in a baking dish and break it up with a fork.

RECOMMENDED PRESERVES: *Runny jellies and faded syrups work best here. If they are of the low-sugar variety, make sure to add extra lemon juice to make up for the lower levels of sweet.*

1 pound/450 g frozen fruit (choose something that goes nicely with your jelly)

1 cup/240 ml runny jelly or syrup

1 tablespoon freshly squeezed lemon or lime juice

Combine the frozen fruit, jelly, and lemon juice in a blender container and blend until well puréed. Taste the purée and add a pinch of sugar, salt, or more lemon juice to adjust the flavors.

Pour the mixture into a low, wide, freezer-safe container. I like using lidded Pyrex baking pans, as they're the right size and there's no risk that you'll spill the granita liquid all over your freezer.

Freeze for 45 to 60 minutes, or until the liquid has begun to harden around the edges, but isn't frozen solid. Using a fork, scrape the granita mixture into flakes and return it to the freezer. Repeat the process of freezing and scraping twice more, until the mixture is completely frozen and is quite dry and flaky. The granita will keep in the freezer for about a week, though you may need to rescrape it before serving.

Jam and Yogurt Pops

When I was a kid, we had a set of ice pop molds. They were made of plastic and had different animals molding into the handles (Raina and I always fought over who would get the lion). We used them to freeze orange or apple juice into pops to bring some relief on hot summer days and thought ourselves lucky to have them.

In recent years, the homemade pop game has changed significantly. There have been a wave of fancy pop makers, as well as gourmet pops and *paletas* coming from both cookbooks and shops. The humble juice pop of my childhood has been left in the dust. Happily, it's not hard to make impressive pops to wow your kids and friends. All you need is a set of molds, a few jars of jam, and some yogurt.

The average mold makes six pops, with each mold holding about 3 ounces/90 ml. I've scaled this formula and the following recipes to produce enough to fill that average set. If your molds take a different volume, you can scale the recipes up or down accordingly.

BASIC JAM AND YOGURT POPS

1 cup/240 ml water
¾ cup/180 ml jam
½ cup/120 ml vanilla yogurt

Combine the water and jam in a blender and blend on low speed until combined. Add the yogurt and blend on low speed until just incorporated.

Pour into your molds, leaving a little space at the top for expansion. Freeze for 5 to 6 hours, or until solid.

To remove the pops from the molds, run them briefly under hot running water until you're able to wiggle them free.

LEMONY PLUM POPS

Blend together ⅞ cup/210 ml of water, 2 tablespoons of freshly squeezed lemon juice, ¾ cup/180 ml of plum jam, and ½ cup/120 ml of lemon yogurt.

SPARKLING GRAPE POPS

Blend together 1 cup/240 ml of sparkling water, ¾ cup/180 ml of grape jam, and ½ cup/120 ml of vanilla yogurt.

DOUBLE STRAWBERRY POPS

Blend together 1 cup/240 ml of water, ¾ cup/180 ml of strawberry jam, and ½ cup/120 ml of strawberry yogurt.
Note: For a more grown-up taste, add 4 to 5 torn basil leaves to the blender along with the yogurt.

ESSENTIAL PRESERVES

While this is very much a book about using up your homemade preserves, it didn't feel like it was right to leave the jams, jellies, pickles, chutneys, relishes, and other preserves entirely out of the game. So, I've rounded up ten of my very favorite preserve recipes into this chapter to serve as a resource. Many of these recipes can be thought of as formulas. This means that you can use the recipe for Berry Jam whether you're working with strawberries, raspberries, or blueberries. The sweet spreads, chutneys, and relishes all yield about 3 pints. The pickles are scaled to produce about a quart. To my mind, that's enough to be the worth the work, but not so much effort that you'll spend all day on a single preserve.

How to Process

The following mini-collection of recipes include some jams and preserves that are designed to be processed in a boiling water bath canner. This is the process in which filled and lidded jars are submerged in a pot of boiling water and boiled for a prescribed amount of time.

The boiling water bath process serves a dual purpose. First, boiling the filled jars kills any microorganisms that might have landed in your jars. Second, the oxygen in the headspace is heated sufficiently to make it expand and vent out of the jar during processing. Once you remove the jar from the hot water, the jar will cool, the space will contract, and the lid will pull down and form a vacuum. This is what keeps your preserves from spoilage.

The Steps

1. If you're starting with brand-new jars, remove their lids and rings. If you're using older jars, check the rims to make sure there are no chips or cracks.

2. Put the rack into the canning pot and put the jars on top.

3. Fill the pot (and jars) with water to cover and bring to a boil. I have found that this is the very easiest way to heat the jars in preparation for canning because you're going to have to heat the canning pot anyway. Why not use that energy to heat the jars as well?

4. While the canning pot comes to a boil, prepare your product.

5. When your recipe is complete, remove the jars from the canning pot, pouring the water back into the pot as you remove the jars, and set them on a clean towel on the counter. There's no need to invert them; the jars will be so hot that any remaining water will rapidly evaporate.

6. Carefully fill the jars with your product, leaving about ¹/₂ inch/1.25 cm of headspace.

7. Wipe the rims of the jar with a clean, damp paper towel or kitchen towel. If the product you're working with is very sticky, you can dip the edge of the cloth in distilled white vinegar for a bit of a cleaning boost.

8. Apply the lids and screw the rings on the jars to hold the lids down during processing. Tighten the bands with the tips of your fingers until they just meet resistance. This is known as "fingertip tight" and twisting to no more than this point will ensure that the air trapped in the jars is able to vent during processing.

9. Carefully lower the filled jars into the canning pot, using canning tongs. You may need to remove some water as you put the jars in the pot, to keep it from overflowing. A heat-resistant measuring cup or a small saucepan with a long handle are good tools for this job.

10. Once the pot has returned to a rolling boil, start your timer. The length of the processing time will vary from recipe to recipe.

11. When your timer goes off, take off the lid and remove the pot from the heat. Let the jars rest for 5 minutes before removing them from the hot water. Gently place them back on the towel-lined countertop and let them cool.

12. The jar lids should begin to ping soon after they've been removed from the pot. The pinging is the sound of the seal forming; the center of the lids will become concave as the vacuum seal takes hold.

13. After the jars have cooled for 24 hours, remove the bands and check the seals. You do this by grasping the jar by the edges of the lid and gently lifting it an inch/2.5 cm or two off the countertop. The lid should hold fast.

14. Once you've determined that your seals are good, you can store your jars in a cool, dark place without the rings for up to 1 year. Any jars with bad seals can still be used provided you catch them within those first 24 hours—just store them in the refrigerator and use within 2 to 3 weeks. You remove the rings because they're no longer necessary and will last longer stored separately from the jars.

Cooking Times

In many of these recipes, I've included suggested cooking times. However, these are just ranges and are not ironclad. Cooking times can vary depending on the humidity in the air, the moisture level in the fruit, the width of your pot, and the intensity of your stove's heat.

It's important to use your judgment when cooking up these sweet preserves and not just depend solely on the suggested cooking times or target temperatures. I always tell my canning students to use all their senses to determine when a preserve is done. You'll see that the surface of the cooking jam will start to look glossier than it did. You can hear that the intensity of the boil gets increasingly frenzied. You can smell how the sugar in the jam starts to take on a toasted fragrance. You can feel how the jam is offering more resistance as you stir. And if you cool down a small spoonful, you can taste how the flavors have married and mellowed. These indicators, along with cooking times and temperature targets, give a fuller picture and help you determine when it's time to take the pot off the heat.

BERRY JAM

MAKES 3 PINT-SIZE/500 ML JARS

This is a basic berry jam that will work with strawberries, raspberries, blueberries, or blackberries. The only berry I can think of that won't work well here is cranberries (they're so tart and full of pectin that it's really best to use them in a recipe dedicated to cranberries).

3 pounds/1.4 kg berries, washed and chopped or smashed
3 tablespoons powdered pectin
3 cups/600 g granulated sugar
Grated zest and juice of 1 lemon

Prepare a boiling water bath and 3 pint-size/500 ml jars according to the process on page 212.

Place the prepared berries in a large, wide, nonreactive pot. Whisk the pectin into the sugar and stir it into the berries. Let it sit for 10 to 15 minutes, or until the sugar has begun to dissolve.

Place the pot on the stove and bring to a boil. Cook the jam over high heat, stirring regularly, for 20 to 25 minutes, or until it begins to thicken, darkens slightly in color, and has reduced in volume by at least one third. Add the lemon zest and juice and stir to incorporate.

When the jam looks glossy, feels thick when you stir, doesn't have a lot of watery liquid separating out, and you're happy with the consistency (and remember that it will thicken as it cools), remove the pot from the heat.

Ladle the jam into the prepared jars, leaving ½ inch/1.25 cm of headspace. Wipe the rims, apply the lids and rings, and process the filled jars in a boiling water bath for 10 minutes.

When the time is up, remove the jars and set them on a folded kitchen towel to cool. When the jars have cooled enough that you can comfortably handle them, check the seals. Sealed jars can be stored at room temperature for up to 1 year. Any unsealed jars should be refrigerated and used promptly.

STONE FRUIT JAM

MAKES 3 PINT-SIZE/500 ML JARS

This basic recipe works well with most stone fruit. I like to peel peaches before turning them into jam, but for all the rest, I leave the skins intact.

4 pounds/960 g apricots, cherries, nectarines, peaches, or plums, pitted and chopped

4 tablespoons powdered pectin

4 cups/800 g granulated sugar

Grated zest and juice of 1 lemon

Prepare a boiling water bath and 3 pint-size/500 ml jars according to the process on page 212.

Place the prepared fruit in a large, wide, nonreactive pot. Whisk the pectin into the sugar and stir it into the fruit. Let it sit for 10 to 15 minutes, or until the sugar has begun to dissolve.

Place the pot on the stove and bring to a boil. Cook the jam over high heat, stirring regularly for 20 to 30 minutes, or until it begins to thicken, darkens slightly in color, and has reduced in volume by at least one third. Add the lemon zest and juice and stir to incorporate.

When the jam looks glossy, feels thick when you stir, doesn't have a lot of watery liquid separating out, and you're happy with the consistency (and remembering that it will thicken as it cools), remove the pot from the heat.

Ladle the jam into the prepared jars, leaving ½ inch/1.25 cm of headspace. Wipe the rims, apply the lids and rings, and process the filled jars in a boiling water bath for 10 minutes.

When the time is up, remove the jars and set them on a folded kitchen towel to cool. When the jars have cooled enough that you can comfortably handle them, check the seals. Sealed jars can be stored at room temperature for up to 1 year. Any unsealed jars should be refrigerated and used promptly.

FRUIT SAUCE

MAKES 3 PINT-SIZE/500 ML JARS

This is basically applesauce, but I want to encourage you to try making it with pears, peaches, or even a combination of fruit. I particularly like a combination of strawberries and apples.

3 pounds/1.4 kg fruit
¼ cup/60 ml water

Prepare a boiling water bath and 3 pint-size/500 ml jars according to the process on page 212.

Prepare the fruit: Peel apples or peaches, hull and crush berries, cut out cores or seeds, remove pits, and finally, roughly chop. Heap the fruit into a large, nonreactive saucepan. Add the water, cover, and bring to a simmer over medium-high heat. Let the fruit cook for 15 to 20 minutes, or until all the pieces are quite tender.

Using a potato masher (chunky!) or immersion blender (smooth!), break down the fruit until it has reached your desired consistency.

Ladle the sauce into the prepared jars, leaving ½ inch/1.25 cm of headspace. Wipe the rims, apply the lids and rings, and process the filled jars in a boiling water bath for 10 minutes.

When the time is up, remove the jars and set them on a folded kitchen towel to cool. When the jars have cooled enough that you can comfortably handle them, check the seals. Sealed jars can be stored at room temperature for up to 1 year. Any unsealed jars should be refrigerated and used promptly.

MARMALADE

MAKES 3 PINT-SIZE/500 ML JARS

This is my basic recipe for homemade marmalade. I've used this same ratio of ingredients for oranges, Meyer lemons, limes, and even grapefruit. The key to success is the overnight soak. It softens the peel and makes for a better finished product.

3 pounds/1.4 kg citrus fruit
  (preferably organic)
6 cups/1.4 L water
6 cups/1.2 kg granulated sugar

Wash the citrus fruit very well. Cut away both the stem and blossom ends of the fruit and slice each fruit into quarters. Cut away the thin strips of white pith from the interior of the wedges and use the tip of your knife to poke out the seeds. Cut each quarter into thin slices from top to bottom. If you're working with very large pieces of fruit, you might want to cut them into eighths rather than quarters.

Once the fruit is sliced, place it into a bowl (along with any of the liquid that you were able to capture) and add the water. Let the sliced fruit soak overnight.

The next day, combine the fruit, soaking water, and sugar in a large, nonreactive pan.

Place the pan on the stove over high heat. Bring the contents of the pot to a boil and cook, stirring regularly, until it has reduced by at least half and is starting to shape up into marmalade. You may need to lower the heat as cooking progresses so that you maintain a low boil without scorching the bottom of the pot.

While the marmalade cooks, prepare a boiling water bath and 3 pint-size/500 ml jars according to the process on page 212. Test for set by checking the temperature of the marmalade. It is finished when it reaches 220°F/104°C and stays there, even when you stir vigorously.

When you determine that the marmalade is done, remove the pot from the heat.

Ladle the marmalade into the prepared jars, leaving ½ inch/1.25 cm of headspace. Wipe the rims, apply the lids and rings, and process the filled jars in a boiling water bath for 10 minutes.

When the time is up, remove the jars and set them

on a folded kitchen towel to cool. When the jars have cooled enough that you can comfortably handle them, check the seals.

Sealed jars can be stored at room temperature for up to 1 year. Any unsealed jars should be refrigerated and used promptly.

TOMATO JAM

MAKES 3 PINT-SIZE/500 ML JARS

This tomato jam is one of the best things I make. It is like the best ketchup you've ever had, but it can also go places that ketchup cannot. Each batch is a labor of love, but is always worth the effort. For a higher yield, use dense tomatoes, such as Roma or San Marzano.

5 pounds/2.3 kg tomatoes, chopped

3½ cups/700 g granulated sugar

½ cup/120 ml bottled lime juice

1 tablespoon grated fresh ginger

1 tablespoon red pepper flakes (use less if you don't like a lot of heat)

2 teaspoons fine sea salt

1 teaspoon ground cinnamon

½ teaspoon ground cloves

Prepare a boiling water bath and 3 pint-size/500 ml jars according to the process on page 212.

Combine the tomatoes, sugar, lime juice, ginger, red pepper flakes, salt, cinnamon, and cloves in a large, nonreactive pot. Bring to a boil over high heat. Once the mixture has reached a hard boil, lower the temperature to medium high.

Stirring regularly, cook the jam at a low boil until it reduces to a sticky, jammy mess. This will take between 1 and 1½ hours, depending on the width of your pot, the amount of water content in the tomatoes, and the temperature at which you are cooking. Watch closely during the final 15 minutes of cooking, because at this point, the jam scorches easily. When the jam is shiny and thick, and doesn't seem to have any watery liquid separating out, remove the pot from the heat.

Ladle the jam into the prepared jars, leaving ½ inch/1.25 cm of headspace. Wipe the rims, apply the lids and rings, and process the filled jars in a boiling water bath for 20 minutes.

When the time is up, remove the jars and set them on a folded kitchen towel to cool. When the jars have cooled enough that you can comfortably handle them, check the seals. Sealed jars can be stored at room temperature for up to 1 year. Any unsealed jars should be refrigerated and used promptly.

ADAPTABLE CHUTNEY

MAKES 3 PINT-SIZE/500 ML JARS

This chutney will work with apples, apricots, cherries, nectarines, peaches, pears, or plums. I typically peel the apples and peaches before stirring them into a batch of chutney, but all the other fruits can keep their skins. Remove pits and cores as needed.

4 pounds/1.8 kg fruit, prepped and chopped

1 medium-size yellow onion, minced

2 cups/340 g golden raisins

1¾ cups/420 ml red wine vinegar

2 cups/440 g packed light brown sugar

1 tablespoon mustard seeds (any color is fine)

1 tablespoon grated fresh ginger

1½ teaspoons fine sea salt

½ teaspoon red pepper flakes

Grated zest and juice of 1 lemon

Combine all the ingredients in a large, nonreactive pot. Bring to a boil over high heat and then lower the heat to medium-high. Cook at a brisk simmer for 45 minutes to an hour, stirring regularly, or until the chutney thickens, darkens, and the flavors start to marry.

While the chutney cooks, prepare a boiling water bath and 3 pint-size/500 ml jars according to the process on page 212.

When the chutney is finished, remove the pot from the heat. Funnel the chutney into the prepared jars, leaving ½ inch/1.25 cm of headspace. Wipe the rims, apply the lids and rings, and process the filled jars in a boiling water bath for 15 minutes.

When the time is up, remove the jars and set them on a folded kitchen towel to cool. When the jars have cooled enough that you can comfortably handle them, check the seals. Sealed jars can be stored at room temperature for up to 1 year. Any unsealed jars should be refrigerated and used promptly.

QUICK CUCUMBER PICKLES

MAKES 1 QUART-SIZE/1 L JAR

This is my favorite way to pickle cucumbers. They taste like a classic dill pickle and retain all their crunch because they go nowhere near a boiling water bath. And they are good with everything from a burger to the fanciest artisanal cheese. I often make a large batch at the end of the season and stash them in the back of the fridge for winter.

2 pounds/900 g pickling
   cucumbers, about 4 inches/
   10 cm long

1 cup/240 ml cider vinegar

1 cup/240 ml water

2 teaspoons fine sea salt

4 garlic cloves, peeled

2 teaspoons dill seeds

1 teaspoon black peppercorns

¼ teaspoon red pepper flakes

Wash and dry the cucumbers. Chop off the ends and slice into spears.

Combine the vinegar, water, and salt in a saucepan and bring to a boil.

Place the garlic cloves, dill seeds, peppercorns, and red pepper flakes in the bottom of a quart-size/1 L jar. Pack the cucumber spears into the jar above the spices tightly, but without crushing them.

Pour the brine into the jar, leaving ¼ inch/6 mm of headspace. Tap the jar gently and wiggle the cucumbers with a wooden chopstick to dislodge any trapped air bubbles. Add more liquid to return the headspace to ¼ inch/6 mm, if necessary. Wipe the rim, apply the lid and ring, and let the jar cool on the countertop. Once it's cool, put the pickles in the refrigerator. Let cure for at least 1 day before eating. The pickles will keep in the fridge for up to 1 month.

KIMCHI

MAKES 1 TO 1½ QUARTS/1 TO 1.5 L KIMCHI

There are countless variations on kimchi in the world. This is simply the approach I take to get close to my favorite store-bought version. It's a good starting place and from here you can improvise and experiment. The only specialty ingredient is the *gochugaru,* which is a Korean chili powder. You can order it online or get it at your local Asian grocery store.

2 pounds/900 g napa cabbage, cut into 2-inch/5 cm chunks

2 tablespoons fine sea salt

8 ounces/225 g daikon radish, julienned

1 bundle green onions, trimmed and cut into 2-inch/5 cm lengths

5 garlic cloves, peeled

1½ inches/4 cm fresh ginger, peeled

1½ teaspoons granulated sugar

2 to 4 tablespoons gochugaru, or to taste

Place the chopped cabbage in a large bowl and add the salt. Use your hands to rub the salt into the cabbage and let it sit overnight.

The next day, rinse the cabbage and let it drain. Return the cabbage to the bowl and add the prepared daikon and green onions.

Place the garlic, ginger, and sugar in a small food chopper or processor. Chop until a paste forms. Add this mixture to the cabbage mixture.

Finally, add the gochugaru. For a batch this size, I like to use 2 tablespoons. That makes a mildly spicy batch. If you're very sensitive to heat, use even less. If you want something with a bit more fire, use the full amount.

Use your hands to work the spices into the vegetables. Pack it all into a half-gallon jar/2 L or small crock. Weigh it down with a 4-ounce/120 ml jar or pickling weights (so that the cabbage stays below the liquid line) and cover the vessel with an airlock or kitchen cloth (the airlock helps keep the sometimes strong fragrance confined).

Let the kimchi ferment for 5 to 6 days, checking every day or two, until you like how it tastes.

When the kimchi is done, portion it into jars and refrigerate. Kept in a tightly closed jar, kimchi will keep in the fridge for up to a year.

PESTO

I make pesto with herbs, such as basil, parsley, or cilantro, as well as flavorful, tender greens, such as arugula, mustard, or young kale. This formula should work regardless of what kind of green you're using as your base. A combination of greens is also nice, particularly if you're trying to stretch a bundle of herbs. As far as the nuts go, I like to use walnuts, cashews, blanched almonds, or pine nuts.

2 cups/40 g packed greens or
  herbs, tough stems removed

½ cup/70 g nuts, toasted

¼ cup/25 g grated Parmesan
  cheese

3 garlic cloves

½ cup/120 ml olive oil, plus more
  if needed to top

Salt and freshly ground black
  pepper

In the work bowl of a food processor, combine the greens, toasted nuts, Parmesan cheese, and garlic. Pulse until a paste begins to form. Remove the lid and scrape down the bowl, if necessary.

Once you've gotten to a chunky paste, slowly stream in the olive oil with the motor running and process until well combined. Taste and add the salt and pepper to taste.

Use the pesto immediately, or pack it into 4-ounce/125 ml freezer-safe containers to preserve for a longer period of time. Top the pesto with a thin layer of olive oil to prevent freezer burn and discoloration. It will keep in the refrigerator for at least 1 week, or in the freezer for up to 1 year.

BASIC SAUERKRAUT

MAKES 1 QUART/1 L SAUERKRAUT

This is the simple sauerkraut that I've used throughout this book. Sometimes I spice it up, or replace some of the cabbage with shredded carrots for a sweeter batch. It's incredibly easy to make and so very satisfying as well!

2 pounds/900 g green cabbage,
  thinly sliced
1 tablespoon fine sea salt

Place the sliced cabbage in large bowl and sprinkle the salt on top. Using your hands, knead the salt into the cabbage, squeezing firmly to help release the liquid from the cabbage.

When the volume of cabbage appears to have reduced by half, pack the salted cabbage into a quart-size/1 L jar in layers, firmly pressing it down with a heavy spoon each time before adding more (all the cabbage should fit into a quart-size/1 L jar).

Press the cabbage down firmly in the jar, so that liquid bubbles up over the surface of the cabbage. Loosely cap the jar, position it on a small saucer or plate, and place it in a cool, dark spot.

Check every other day, removing any surface scum that forms and pressing cabbage down if it has floated above the liquid. Be warned that sauerkraut can get a little stinky. It's normal for it to smell like sweaty feet. However, if it starts to smell fishy or like rotten eggs, something has gone wrong. This happens rarely, but does occasionally occur. If your sauerkraut spoils or develops pink mold, throw it out.

After a week, taste the sauerkraut. If you like the flavor, place the jar in the refrigerator. If you want something a bit stronger, let it continue to ferment until it pleases you. Kept in a tightly closed jar, sauerkraut will keep in the fridge for up to a year.

ACKNOWLEDGMENTS

AS IS ALWAYS THE CASE WITH CREATIVE WORKS, THE MAKING of this book was not a solitary effort. It was shaped, tested, edited, photographed, and made beautiful by a cast of many, and I am forever grateful to the people who have helped me bring it out of my head and into the world.

I had two editors work on this book and I am thankful for them both. Kristen Green Wiewora is my longtime editor and it is always a delight to collaborate with a dear friend. Kristen went out on maternity leave in the midst of this book (welcome to the world, Rose!) and her colleague Jordana Tusman stepped into the fray.

A river of thanks goes to my agent, Clare Pelino. I am so lucky to have her shrewd intelligence and deep kindness on my side.

This book would not have made it to its deadline without help from freelance editor, recipe developer, food writer, and dear friend, Emily Teel. She leapt into the chaos during the last eight weeks of the drafting process and saved me from a meltdown. She made sense of tester feedback, developed a handful of cocktails, gave me honest feedback about recipes that weren't making the cut, and sorted through my messy spreadsheet to help me find the path toward the finish line.

Big thanks to Amanda Richmond for her gorgeous design work. Steve Legato, thank you for your artistry with lights and lenses. Erin McDowell, I am so grateful that we finally got to work together. Thank you for sharing your food styling talent with me. Thanks also go to Evan Coben for all her hard photo shoot work.

I have nothing but appreciation and gratitude for my husband and fellow writer, Scott McNulty. His steadfast, loving belief in me keeps me moving forward, even when I fear I've tumbled off the path.

My gratitude for my parents, Leana and Morris McClellan, is unending. They helped me brainstorm flavor combinations, provided suggestions for headnotes when I didn't think I had any more stories to tell, and read every word of this book in early draft form. I am truly the luckiest.

To my sister Raina Rose and brother-in-law Andrew Pressman. I am so grateful to have you both as family and fellow travelers on this creative path. Also, thanks for bringing Emmett and Benny into the world. They are fun, lovely, crazy-making boys and I am so happy to be their aunt.

Many thanks go to my team of volunteer recipe testers. They were instrumental in making sure that the dishes in this book would work on every stove and in every kitchen. They are Genevieve Boehme, Abby Doyle, Margo Gillaspy, Jen Wetzel, Michele Knaub, Rebecca Gagnon, Jamie Png, Chrissy Bellizzi, Casey DelliCarpini, Jackie Botto, Angelica Jaszek, Christina Bello, Kelly Schultz Skupnik, Meryl Carver-Allmond, Jenny Pierce, and Heidi Bahr.

I am so lucky to have a collective of friends and colleagues both near and far, to whom I can turn when I am stuck, uncertain, overwhelmed, or momentarily fed up. They include Kate Payne, Deena Prichep, Joy Manning, Molly Watson, Maggie Battista, Meg Brown, Sean Timberlake, Joel MacCharles, Dana Harrison, Julia Sforza, Shae Irving, Kaela Porter, Seth Carrier-Ladd, Cindy McCauley, Ingrid Moeller, Andrea Baxter, Roz Duffy, Janet Reich Elsbach, Ivy Manning, Alana Chernila, Ashley English, Audra Wolfe, Tenaya Darlington, Alexis Siemons, and Amanda Feifer. Thank you all.

Finally, my infinite thanks go out to the community of home cooks and canners who read the blog, come to my classes, use my recipes, and share their many preserving successes. You all are the reason I do what I do.

INDEX